MW00453383

Collector's Encyclopedia of
BLACK DOLLS

By
Patikii & Tyson Gibbs

COLLECTOR BOOKS
A Division of Schroeder Publishing Co., Inc.

The current values in this book should be used only as a guide. They are not intended to set prices, which vary from one section of the country to another. Auction prices as well as dealer prices vary greatly and are affected by condition as well as demand. Neither the Author nor the Publisher assumes responsibility for any losses that might be incurred as a result of consulting this guide.

On the cover:

Maker's Name: Schoenau & Hoffmeister
Marks: S ("PB" in a star) H
Origin: Germany
Size: 26″
Date: Purchased circa 1914
Description: Brown bisque socket head with brown porcelain eyes and porcelain upper teeth on a fully ball jointed wood and composition body. Black human hair wig (original). Wearing a white handmade dress originally worn by her owner as a child. Excellent condition. This doll was purchased by the owner's father from the National Baptist Publishing Board in Nashville, Tennessee. Dr. R.H. Boyd, head of the board, was a Black entrepreneur, who among other things, produced and marketed Black dolls and doll bodies for imported bisque heads.
Courtesy of: Mrs. Ruth Martha Caulder-Grant and family
Price Range: $1,100.00-1,400.00

Additional copies of this book may be ordered from:

Collector Books
P.O. Box 3009
Paducah, KY 42001

@$14.95. Add $2.00 for postage and handling.

Copyright: Patikii & Tyson Gibbs, 1987
Updated Values 1989

This book or any part thereof may not be reproduced without the written consent of the Author and Publisher.

Acknowledgements

We wish to give a very special thanks to those individuals, businesses and museums that made this book possible. Without their support and generous sharing of their time, places and dolls, this book would not have been possible. We would also like to thank doll collectors in the Nashville, Tennessee area who wish to remain anonymous.

Angie's Doll Boutique (Private Collection)
Alexandria, VA

Aspen Historical Society
Aspen, CO

Ron Carr Collection

Christie's East
New York, NY

Marvin Cohen Doll Auctions
New Lebanon, NY

DAR Museum
Washington, D.C.

Melva Davern Collection

Dolly Wares Doll Museum
Florence, OR

Fairhaven Doll Museum

The Good Fairy Doll Museum/Elizabeth Connors
Cranford, NJ

Evelyn Heidepriem Collection

LaShawne High Collection

Hudson River Museum
Yonkers, NY

Iowa State Historical Department
Des Moines, IA

Winnie Lee Collection
Camarillo, CA

Lightner Museum
St. Augustine, FL

Meme's Dolls
Alabama/Birmingham

The Paper Pile
San Anselmo, CA

DeLois Sellers Collection

Silver Springs (Museum)
Silver Springs, FL

Sotheby's
New York, NY

The Stamford Historical Society
Stamford, CT

Charlene Upham Antiques
Mardela Springs, MD

Wenham Historical Association and Museum, Inc.

Whiteway Antique Mall
Nashville, TN

Peggy Williams Collection

Yarmouth County Museum
Nova Scotia Canada

Yesteryears Museum
Sandwich, MA

Dedication

This book is dedicated to collectors of all ages that have searched patiently for the dolls of color included in this book.

Contents

Introduction

Early Years

In the United States, the doll making industry of the 17th, 18th and early 19th century paralleled the development of other "arts" in America. That is, in the city individuals often had more time to have different individuals participate in specialized industries. Outside the city, more often than not, many of the people were engaged in making a living to the extent that the "arts" were part of the day to day culture. Thus, in the early years of America, the city and countryside living activities were indistinguishable. As time passed, and the cities grew, there was a clear distinction between those decorative arts made by city aritsans and those made by the small town dwellers. The creation of the Black doll was part of this development in the arts.

During the time period between the late 1600 and the early 1800s, the major doll making activity was centered around individual doll artisans and unskilled persons who worked to develop what they felt. The Black dolls of this period, when such is available, will usually be made of cloth, wood, tobacco leaves, cornhusks and other such readily available materials. The images on the dolls will be closely aligned with the occupations of the Blacks - "mammys", slaves, servants, etc. There were a few doll makers who made dolls which did not fit the typical Black doll-type of the period--Joel Ellis, Mason and Taylor--to name a few. Both Black and White artisans made these dolls and without documentation, there really is no way to distinguish dolls made by slaves, Black Freedmen, country artisans and others. However, many such claims are made to the contrary.

Elsewhere around the world, during this same time period, the Black dolls represented similar figures with the exception of an occasional creche figure of a Black person. It must be remembered that Europe is much older than the United States and by the mid to late 19th century, the doll had become a sophisticated toy. For example, in France, Italy and Britain, dolls were being automated. A few of these dolls from France, circa 1800-1850, were Black figures of exceptional craftsmanship now selling for thousands of dollars. In Africa, most of the doll figurines were utilitarian reflecting the use of these images for various ceremonial purposes. Such figurines are considered to be "African Folk Art" and play a very limited role in the American Doll Collecting field. In places such as Australia and South Africa the few images available of Black dolls were created to reflect the local native population. During these early years, there is very little evidence that Japan or Mexico created dolls which were Black.

In terms of quality, much of it has to be "in the eye of the beholder". These early dolls from almost all of the countries (with the exception of the French dolls and some German dolls) are crudely-made objects with a kind of rustic charm, popular with many collectors of "Folk Art". These items usually are used as decorative pieces around the home. A few may be part of a larger collection of Black memorabilia and others may be found among an eclectic doll collector's treasures, having samples from all eras.

Late 19th and Early 20th Century

Between 1850 and 1920, individual doll makers, doll artists and small companies were producing most of the dolls being made in America. There were dolls and doll parts sold in America which were imported from countries such as Germany and France. These dolls and parts represented few Black dolls and since only a small percentage of all dolls assembled or sold in America during this period were Black, a shortage of these dolls existed then and are in shortage now.

During the 1920s, when the American doll making industry moved toward full mass production, an increase in the number of Black dolls became evident. Some companies, such as the Allied Grand Doll manufacturing company, of Brooklyn, New York, boasted about being, ". . . Headquarters for Colored Babies", as stated in the 1937 *Playthings Directory*. This company, along with a few others, was a leader in making Black dolls. The dolls being sold were made of composition and sold for less than two or three dollars. Among others, the Horsman Doll Company, Amberg Dolls, Arcy, A&H, Effanbee and Ideal represent only a partial listing of the large, creative, aggressive and competitive companies which made Black dolls.

In the 1944-45 issue of the *Playthings Directory* (which listed companies and their ads for the doll and toy industry), another company in New York City was listed as specializing solely in Black dolls, the Lujon Sun Tan-Colored Doll Company. Although there were many doll companies producing Black dolls, there were few available in the stores or on display. One can only guess, that perhaps, the store owners felt that they would offend its non-Black patrons if too many of the brown-colored dolls were displayed. The Black doll not only represented the subject which it was modeled after but also the social and cultural status of Black people in America. Prior to the early 1950s many Black people did not or were not allowed to freely mingle with Whites in this country and it would stand to reason that the Black dolls would not be openly displayed in large quantities. The ironic thing about this situation is that more Whites than Blacks bought the Black doll. Again, following the times, more Whites could afford the Black dolls (or any dolls) than could a Black person, who often times lived on a modest income prior to the 1950s. The other possibility is that Blacks did not like the dolls that were made to represent them because most of the dolls were done in caricature form or had non-ethnic features. Those dolls which had ethnic features from Germany or France were very expensive for the time and were considered luxury items which most Blacks could not afford.

Modern Times

The dawn of the civil rights movement during the 1950s brought about a change in America. The American people of the two major races (Blacks and Whites) both wanted a better quality of life after experiencing a recent war (World War II) and the Korean Conflict. The image of the Black race had not been very positive before the onset of this movement which promoted a concerned image of Black people. This public makeover was already evidenced in the doll industry on a moderate scale. Psychological research studies showed that Black children were most affected by the lack of positive imagery and thus more persons began to address the problem of imagery-perception. One such individual was Sarah Lee Creech, a concerned Black lady who developed an idea to have a series of ethnically-correct dolls created in the image of the Black race. It is not known if Ms. Creech was aware that such dolls were already being made by a few doll companies, but she carried through with her plans and developed one such doll. A doll artist, Sheila Burlingame, was chosen to design the doll and the name "Sara(h) Lee" was given to her creation. This project had the endorsement of such influential and affluent people as: Mrs. Eleanor Roosevelt; Dr. Ralph Bunche, director of the United Nations Department of Trusteeship; Walter White, executive director of the National Association for the Advancement of Colored People; and numerous other leaders. Credit was given to this effort in an issue of the 1952 *Life Magazine*. It stated:

> At an early age U.S. Negro children have had their many disadvantages illustrated for them by one fact: there has never been a doll they could call their own. They have always had to play with unsatisfactory "pickaninny" dolls or dolls painted brown. But recently Sarah Lee Creech of Belle · Glade, Florida, reflecting on that fact, decided to have a doll made that would be anthropologically correct and something a Negro child could be proud of. The result is the first truly Negro doll ever made. The dolls were made of vinylite plastic, have eyes which move and are a dark brown in color. Stores selling the new dolls report that they are almost as popular with the white children as with colored.

The collaboration of Ms. Creech and Mrs. Burlingame was unusual but not totally unique or new. During this same period many companies such as the Horsman Doll Company were also commissioning doll artists to create Black dolls with ethnically correct features. Polly and Pete, circa 1950, are two such dolls. During this time businesses became aware of the demand for positive Black subjects portrayed on consumable goods, and doll companies competed to fill the demand.

In the 1960s a company called the Shandanna Doll and Toy Company was founded. Their specialty was creating Black dolls and learning toys. Of particular interest is their creation of ethnically correct dolls in both vinyl and cloth. The major target group for their items was not the collectors however, but children and juveniles. Thus, for the most part, many of Shandanna's dolls did not survive the rough and tumble of children at play. Other popular dolls made during the early 1960s such as the Barbie family, the Sasha family and large walking dolls made by such companies as Ideal and Uneeda were occassionally created in Black images. Popular during this time also, was the importation of modern African dolls, Jamaican dolls, Trinidadian Islands' dolls as well as individual Doll Artist creations. Many Blacks in America became doll artisans and this contributed to the variety of Black dolls on the market at the time.

In the 1970s and 1980s several trends have emerged for the Black doll, they include but are not limited to:

1. smaller companies and doll artisans making Black dolls;
2. the resurgence of folk dolls being made in places such as Tennessee, Georgia, Louisiana and Alabama. These dolls are usually replicas of the "mammy" type dolls of the early 1900s;
3. the increased popularity of all types of Black dolls for the collector. What has not emerged during the 1970s and 1980s is the larger doll companies creating unique, ethnically correct dolls for the public at large.

The three trends listed above, in fact, illustrate the diversity of the Black doll market during this time period. The first market is illustrated by those persons who collect mainly new dolls but want something which is unique. These individuals tend to buy from the many doll artisans who advertise in the doll-trade magazines and papers. The second market is represented by those persons who want to buy decorative items as a part of the increased interest in "Early Americana", and therefore are attracted to modern folk art which often includes cloth and wooden Black dolls. The third market is representative of those individuals who want to own true early folk art, not replicas, as part of their collection of early Americana. These individuals have the hardest times finding true old pieces, because in many instances, using old cloth, modern artisans fashion "new" dolls to look old.

There is always the ever present fourth market which represents part of the increased interest in doll collecting in general, whereby individual collectors of dolls purchase collectible Black dolls made prior to the 1960 as part of their overall doll collection. These individuals are not part of the changes that have taken place in the modern doll market. That is, they are not part of any past or present fads but, rather they represent the core of doll collectors of both Black and White dolls. In fact, many doll companies today claim that while Black dolls sell at a steady pace, the market for new Black dolls has not increased over the past decade. This is not so with older collectible Black dolls, regardless of cost. Most dealers in dolls report scarcities and high demand of the older collectible Black dolls.

Scarcity of the Black Doll

The increased popularity of the "Black" doll today and the rising number of doll collectors contributes to the scarcity of the Black doll. Black dolls have always been considered unique. When the additional time was taken to create a Black doll with Negroid features, the rewards were usually great for its creator. The Black doll has attracted adults and children alike of all cultures. A Black "Creche" figure for example, was highly sought after by many individuals during the 19th century who wanted to add variety to their exhibits of religious nativity scenes. These figures were rare during this time period because they were often only made by request. The mammy doll during the early 1900s was also popular and for the most part was handmade until the doll industry seized its popularity and began to make them by the thousands (particularly paper and cloth materials). Although the mammy doll was made by the thousands, it is scarce in the doll market today. In the main, when these dolls were created, they were meant to be played with and were often passed down from child to child, eventually becoming totally worn and discarded.

Black dolls made of materials such as wood, corn shucks or kelp were made in small quantities and have gained popularity over the years, thus making them harder to find. Dolls made of these materials described above and the early handmade rag (mammy) dolls are also a part of the folk art made in America's earlier years. Folk art of any kind in America today is highly demanded by the public. The combination of being both folk art and a Black doll has created an even higher demand for these dolls which are often also bought by non-doll collectors as decorative pieces. When a large number of White dolls were being created in expensive materials such as china and bisque a smaller number of Black dolls were also created in the same materials. These brown-colored dolls can be found dressed in silks as fashion dolls, kings, servants, children, babies and occupational dolls such as nuns or musicians. Since a fewer number of the Black dolls were created and the demand often exceeded the supply, they were sought after and they are a premium today. By the time the revolutionary material called "composition" compound was being fashioned into dolls, the doll industry was capable of producing thousands of dolls daily.

The bulk of the collectible Black dolls was manufactured between 1900 and 1950, and with an unceasing demand for them, the manufacturers began to carry full lines of these dolls with varying features and skin tones. Prior to the 1920s, Germany, France and England were the leaders in the doll industry. The dolls from these countries were made of bisque china and composition. They supplied other countries with dolls including a fair portion of the dolls available on the American market. Also on the American market, made of a lesser quality, but using the same materials were dolls imported from Japan. By the 1920s American doll companies began to flourish. Most of the Black dolls made in other countries were designed to appeal to the varied tastes of their buyers. Often times these dolls were shipped undressed and upon arrival they were then dressed. This method of obtaining dolls lends an interesting twist in the collectibles field. One will find that many tourist dolls in various costumes can be traced to countries such as Germany, France and England. Brown-colored dolls may often have features identical to those of white dolls (as mentioned earlier) and merely be attired in their native country's costume. When manufacturers in the United States became major suppliers in the doll industry during the 1920s they began to produce Black dolls by similar methods used in other countries. These methods included merely painting White dolls black or brown in addition to using the technique of creating molds which represented Black people with more naturalistic features (often referred to as negroid features).

Black dolls which have negroid features are often times more desirable to collectors than are those merely painted brown. The dolls with negroid features are more appealing and appear to be more natural looking. This added feature for the Black doll is not unlike the appeal that a White doll may have had with rosy cheeks and an olive complexion in comparison to those with a pale white color and the cheeks not accented. Most Black dolls are chosen by collectors for their appeal as well as their historic attributes. When a Black doll is chosen by a collector it is usually for its ethnic appeal. Brown paint applied to the faces of White dolls produces a very pleasant looking doll but it is more easily obtained than a doll that has had a specific mold created with ethnic features. When the added step of designing a special mold for a Black doll was taken, it usually required the skills of a doll artist either working alone or jointly with a doll company. There were many doll artists employed by the American doll companies during the 1920s. The dolls produced by this joint venture were called "Artists Dolls". The doll artists would use live models, sketching the features of the person and then they carefully designed their molds. As you might expect, Black dolls with ethnic features are scarce.

What does all the above mean in terms of the availability of the Black doll? It means that although old Black dolls in early materials were made in small quantities they are, however, still available. Dolls made of composition were made in large quantities and they are readily available. Dolls made of china and bisque were made in small quantities and are scarce. Even more scarce are dolls made of wood and cloth made prior to 1850. Celluloid dolls in Black, of quality, are rare; however, those of inferior quality are readily available. Rubber, wax and papier mache dolls of any type are scarce and this is particularly so with the Black dolls. Vinyl and plastic dolls made after 1950 are very common for both Black and White dolls.

One of the major issues which has to be addressed by the collector, in terms of the scarcity of the Black doll, is "who actually made the doll in question". For most Black dolls--that is, dolls made in materials such as rubber, vinyl, plastic and composition--one can safely assume that these dolls, although often unmarked, were usually made by a manufacturing company. Dolls of bisque, china and papier mache can usually be attributed to a manufacturing company. One must bear in mind, however, that many individual doll artisans (Black and White) used these materials to create their dolls. Of particular concern to collectors, should be the dolls of materials such as tobacco leaves, kelp and cloth. These materials, when used to make Black dolls are often attributed to either Black artisans or slaves. While many Black artisans and slaves did create dolls, the quantity of handmade dolls available precludes them all, being made by a Black person. It must be remembered that the attribution of a Black doll to a Black artisan, without documentation, will unreasonably increase the price of the doll. In addition such attribution may be accompanied by words such as scarce, rare, unique, unusual, etc., for a doll which is not all of these things.

Price of the Black Doll

Previously it has been noted that older Black dolls are not plentiful for obvious reasons such as: small quantities were originally produced; small quantities were readily available at local stores; and many were destroyed by children at play. In light of the fact that these dolls are scarce it would stand to reason that they are also expensive when found. The cost factor has been present since the beginning of their production. It was costly to add the needed coloring for their complexions and later to employ the doll artists to create special molds. Since only a small number of the total dolls produced daily were Black, this caused a shortage in the market, resulting in an increase in the price. When observing the re-sell market of these dolls one will notice that the words "hard to find", "rare" and "unusual" are usually accompanied by a higher price tag. The general trend throughout the doll history has been that male dolls are considered rare and the Black male doll is even rarer, especially if they are of an exceptional quality.

The doll market has changed tremendously over the last two decades. It was not until the onset of the 1960s that doll collecting in America became fashionable and very popular. Some of the first doll clubs began to form in America and rare and beautiful dolls could be bought for a mere fraction of today's market value. An excellent example is the Shirley Temple doll made during the 1930s which was widely mass produced in America and abroad, could be bought during the 1960s for approximately $50. Today, twenty plus years later, Shirley Temple dolls range from $200 to $800. A rare Hawaiian Shirley Temple with brown skin is too rare to compute an accurate price range on today's open market. The prices of old Black dolls have increased steadily with the increase in prices of all dolls and more recently older Black dolls have been averaging 10 percent or higher, than the non-Black doll of the same or a similar type. When attempting to price Black dolls for sale or purchasing purposes the 10 percent and higher formula is a good measure to follow.

The prices of Black dolls will vary in different regions of the United States. The formula mentioned in the above paragraph will hold true in any region. Black dolls made prior to the 19th century are usually found in museums and they are extremely expensive. Dolls made during this time period sell for thousands of dollars and often times their prices exceed $10,000. During the 19th century more doll companies were established and thus increased the number of Black dolls being made. Today, these 19th century dolls sell for as much as the earlier decorative dolls because of their refined and exquisite quality. The dolls in question can be found bearing foreign and/or American marks of identity. In recent years a popular foreign doll of the 19th century by the Bru Doll Company of France has been selling for over five figures. These dolls are well executed. Other doll companies abroad and in America made millions of well-made dolls during the 19th century but few can command the same prices as the Bru or Jumeau dolls, or other small French doll companies. The Black Jumeau doll varies in price depending on their execution and the materials of which it was made. The Black Bru, however, is always a highly-prized and highly-priced doll. The inumerable other black dolls made during this period usually sell for between $300 and $1000.

By the 20th century the industrial revolution in the United States is viewed as having a strong but mixed impact on the doll industry. Millions of dolls were being mass produced. Some of the dolls were well executed, whereas others were not. The well-made dolls command a handsome price in the upper hundreds and the ones of lesser quality may sell for less than $100. Black dolls made during the same time period, early 1900s, will follow the usual 10 percent plus formula set forth above. Most dolls made by doll artists will sell for slightly more than a mass-produced doll, and again, the Black doll will be even more expensive. As mentioned earlier in this book, the 1950s prompted many companies and doll artists to increase the production of Black dolls.

Today, the collector will do well to trade with dealers that specialize in dolls. They are usually more informed than the dealer that occassionally sells dolls. Another source of information is the variety of price guides to dolls such as *Doll Values* by Patricia Smith; *Price Guide to Dolls* by Robert W. Miller; *The Blue Book of Dolls and Values* series by Jan Foulke; *The Warner Collector's Guide to Dolls* by Jean Bach; and *Horsman Dolls, 1950-1970* by Patikii Gibbs. These are a sampling of books that can help you with determining a fair price and provide you with a time frame from which to work with while researching the Black doll in question. While these books are helpful, they are merely guides in determining prices. Price guides generally give an overall price range based on and taking into consideration the price differences in the various regions of the country (USA).

BLACK DOLL NETWORKS
107 2nd Ave. N., Suite 7
Nashville, TN 37201

Vinyl, Plastic,

Rubber & Celluloid Dolls

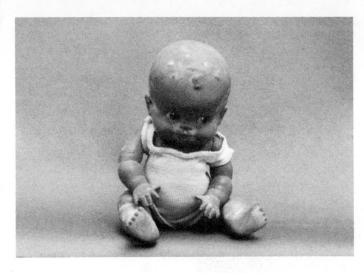

Name: Amosandra
Maker's Name: Columbia Broadcasting System, Inc. (Sun Rubber Co.)
Marks: COLUMBIA BROADCASTING SYSTEM, INC. DESIGNED BY RUTH E. NEWTON/MFD. BY/THE SUN RUBBER CO./BARBERTON, O. USA/PAT. 2118682/PAT. 2160739
Origin: U.S.A.
Size: 10″
Date: ©1950s
Description: Medium brown fully jointed vinyl, brown painted eyes, molded nose and mouth with hole and tongue showing, molded deeply curled hair. Doll squeaks when squeezed. Original jumpsuit. *Some dolls may be dressed in a diaper an shirt. Good condition.
Comments: This doll was designed to represent the child of the famous Amos 'n Andy broadcasting family.
Courtesy of: Silver Springs "Museum"
Price Range: $60.00-80.00

Name: "No Name" Male Boy
Maker's Name: Australia (no company name)
Marks: AUSTRAILIA
Origin: Australia
Size: 10″
Date: circa 1930s-1950s
Description: Hard black plastic male toddler with brown plastic sleep eyes, molded Negroid features, fully jointed with short curly fleeced hair. All original. Excellent condition. *Burlap waist-wrap has animal teeth attached to the front.
Comments: Available
Courtesy of: Silver Springs "Museum"
Price Range: $50.00-70.00

Name: "No Name" Male Boy
Maker's Name: P.M.I. / I K J (on the back)
Marks: P.M.I. / I K J
Origin: Attributed to Australian
Size: 4″
Date: circa 1940s-1950s
Description: Hard plastic black, fully jointed, molded face and body. All original animal fur head dress and skirt with beads on the arms, neck, waist and ankles. Excellent condition.
Comments: Available but not plentiful.
Courtesy of: Dolly Wares Doll Museum
Price Range: $60.00-75.00

Name: Bride
Maker's Name: Goodyear Rubber Co.
Marks: GOODYEAR
Origin: U.S.A.
Size: 27″
Date: circa 1940s
Description: Hard rubber very light brown color, jointed at the arms. Finely detailed molded features, synthetic wig. Dressed in original fine lace dress, original silk floral bouquet. This light complexioned doll may have been a model doll. All original. Excellent condition.
Comments: Extremely well made doll. Available but not plentiful.
Courtesy of: Dolly Wares Doll Museum
Price Range: $250.00-300.00

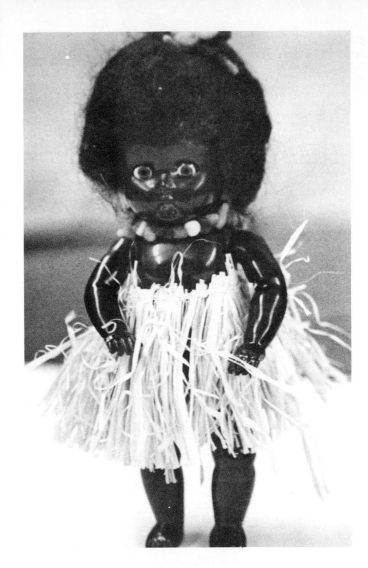

Name: "No Name" Female Girl
Maker's Name: Australia (no company name)
Marks: MADE IN AUSTRALIA
Origin: Australia
Size: 6"
Date: circa 1940s
Description: Hard plastic brown fully jointed, fuzzy reddish black mohair wig, brown sleep eyes. All original grass skirt and head decorations/necklace. Excellent condition.
Comments: Available
Courtesy of: Dolly Wares Doll Museum
Price Range: $50.00-65.00

Name: "No Name"
Maker's Name: Unmarked
Marks: None
Origin: U.S.A.
Size: 2½"
Date: circa 1880-1900
Description: Grayish/brown gutta-percha child doll with molded painted features. Good condition.
Comments: Rare material which doll artists and companies discontinued its use because of the fast deterioration. Scarce material/common style.
Courtesy of: Yesteryear's Museum
Price Range: $60.00-70.00

Name: "No Name" Female Body
Maker's Name: Horsman Dolls, Inc.
Marks: HORSMAN DOLL MFG. CO., A/HORSMAN/DOLL, HORSMAN, IRENE SZOR/HORSMAN (or) Horsman Dolls, Inc.
Origin: U.S.A.
Size: 15″, 17″, 19″, 21″ & 25″
Date: circa 1940s-1950s
Description: Soft vinylite brand plastic arms and legs, cotton-stuffed cloth bodies, glassine brown sleep eyes, open mouth with teeth and tongue or closed mouth, mohair wig or molded tinted hair, crying voice box. Excellent condition.
Comments: Available
Price Range: $155.00-175.00

Name: Tynie Baby *Special Tynie Baby
Maker's Name: Horsman Dolls, Inc.
Marks: HORSMAN DOLL MFG. CO., A/HORSMAN/DOLL, HORSMAN, IRENE SZOR/HORSMAN (or) Horsman Dolls, Inc.
Origin: U.S.A.
Size: 15″ & 20″
Date: circa 1950s
Description: Soft vinylite brand plastic head, arms and legs, cotton-stuffed cloth body, painted eyes, open mouth with tongue showing, hand-painted newborn features, voice box "crying" sound or *1 minute crying stops when picked up (20″ size only). Medium brown color. Cotton flannel blanket tied with large satin ribbon and/or embroidered pillow or none. Excellent condition.
Comments: Tynie Baby was first created in the early 1900s by E.I. Horsman (early Horsman Dolls, Inc. Company). The first Tynie Baby was an all bisque baby. The doll is being made today in a soft vinyl (all vinyl).
Price Range: $140.00-175.00

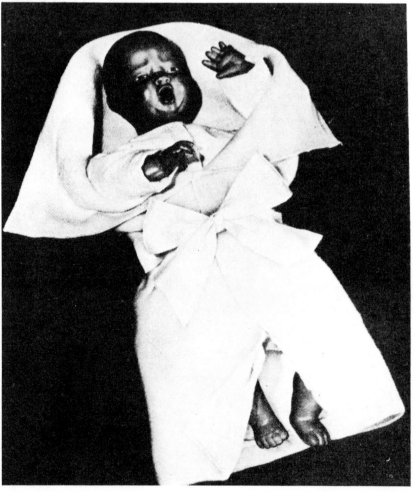

Name: "No Name" Female Toddler
Maker's Name: Horsman Dolls, Inc.
Marks: HORSMAN DOLL MFG. CO., A/HORSMAN/DOLL, HORSMAN, IRENE SZOR/HORSMAN (or) Horsman Dolls, Inc.
Origin: U.S.A.
Size: 16″, 18″, 20″, 22″ & 25″
Date: circa 1950s
Description: Soft brown vinyl plastic, brown glassine eyes, closed mouth, turning head, black painted hair or black rooted curly short dynel fiber hair, voice box with a "coo" sound. All original. Vinyl curlers with instructions for curling. Excellent condition.
Comments: Horsman made large quantities of "No Name" dolls of quality. The company was a leader in producing Black dolls. *Composition dolls with similar features were made during the 1940s and 1930s.
Price Range: $160.00-175.00

Name: Fairy Skin Baby
Maker's Name: Horsman Dolls, Inc.
Marks: HORSMAN DOLL MFG. CO., A/HORSMAN/DOLL, HORSMAN, IRENE SZOR/HORSMAN (or) Horsman Dolls, Inc.
Origin: U.S.A.
Size: 13″, 15″, 17″, 19″, 21″, 23″ & 25″
Date: circa 1940s-1950s
Description: Soft vinyl Fairy Skin of a warm brown tone, painted molded features, turning head, "coos" when squeezed, high facial cheeks, Negroid features, closed mouth and black Saran hair. All original. Excellent condition.
Comments: 1940s dolls may be made of composition or rubber.
Price Range: $185.00-220.00

Name: Baby Precious
Maker's Name: Horsman Dolls, Inc.
Marks: HORSMAN DOLL MFG. CO., A/HORSMAN/DOLL, HORSMAN, IRENE
SZOR/HORSMAN (or) Horsman Dolls, Inc.
Origin: U.S.A.
Size: 11″, 13″, 15″, 17″, 19″, *23″, *25″ & 8″ baby
Date: circa 1950s
Description: Soft vinyl brown head, glassine brown sleep eyes, closed mouth, super-
flex arms and legs or *jointed arms. Black short curly hair, voice box with a "coo"
sound, doll may come alone or with a smaller doll in arms (8″ baby). All original.
Excellent condition.
Comments: Doll also available from the 1960s in an all vinyl jointed style.
Price Range: $125.00-145.00

Name: Cindy Strutter Bride
Maker's Name: Horsman Dolls, Inc.
Marks: HORSMAN DOLL MFG. CO., A/HORSMAN/DOLL, HORSMAN, IRENE
SZOR/HORSMAN (or) Horsman Dolls, Inc.
Origin: U.S.A.
Size: 14″, 16″, 18″ & 24″
Date: circa 1940s-1950s
Description: Brown vinyl bride doll with jointed arms, rooted long black Saran curled hair,
voice box with "coo" sound, glassine brown sleep eyes. Doll walks when you hold her
hand and lead her. Accessories include comb, brush, curlers, mirror, vinyl purse, wire
hangers, wardrobe trunk with handle or NONE or a floral bouquet only. All original.
Excellent condition.
Comments: Bride dolls have always been popular and sought after. Black bride dolls made
by large doll companies prior to the 1970s are available but not plentiful.
Price Range: $175.00-195.00

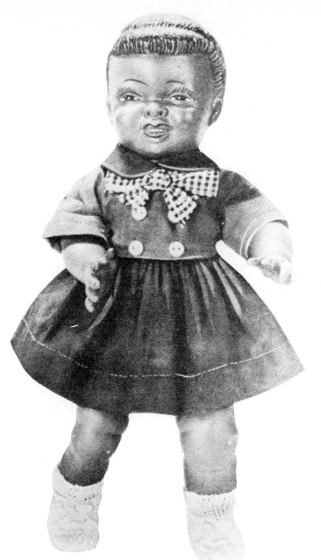

Name: Polly and Pete

Maker's Name: Horsman Dolls, Inc.

Marks: HORSMAN DOLL MFG. CO., A/HORSMAN/DOLL, HORSMAN, IRENE SZOR/HORSMAN (or) Horsman Dolls, Inc.

Origin: U.S.A.

Size: 13″

Date: circa 1956-1958

Description: Brown vinyl twins with strong Negroid features rendered in a naturalistic manner. Deeply molded curled hair for the male doll and bangs and ponytail for the female. Hair is delicately tinted black. Both dolls have painted brown eyes, open mouth with teeth, dusky complexion, super-flex legs, turning heads, voice boxes with "coo" sounds. Smiling expressions.

Comments: Polly and Pete were only made a short time period. Scarce. Artist dolls molded from live subjects.

Price Range: $300.00-400.00 pair

17

Name: Peggy Ann (Sub-teen Doll)
Maker's Name: Horsman Dolls, Inc.
Marks: HORSMAN DOLL MFG. CO., A/HORSMAN/DOLL, HORSMAN, IRENE SZOR/HORSMAN (or) Horsman Dolls, Inc.
Origin: U.S.A.
Size: 12", *15", 17" & 19"
Date: circa 1950s-1960s
Description: Brown vinyl fully jointed, slim legs, rooted black hair with a ponytail and sculpted features, glassine brown eyes and closed mouth. Accessories include a *school bag attached to wrist, brush, mirror, snap-lock suitcase with handle or No Accessories. All original. Excellent condition.
Comments: Available. Doll above was made in 1959.
Price Range: $100.00-125.00

Name: Love-Me Baby
Maker's Name: Horsman Dolls, Inc.
Marks: HORSMAN DOLL MFG. CO., A/HORSMAN/DOLL, HORSMAN, IRENE SZOR/HORSMAN (or) Horsman Dolls, Inc.
Origin: U.S.A.
Size: 11", 13", 15", 17", 19", 21", 23" & 25"
Date: circa 1950s-1960s (vinyl Fairy Skin - only)
Description: Brown vinyl Fairy Skin doll with super-flex bendable legs, voice box "coo" sound, turning head, rooted black hair in a ponytail and bangs. Doll may come with a snap-lock suitcase with a handle, soap, sponge, plastic curlers, brush, comb, mirror and hangers or NO ACCESSORIES. All original. Excellent condition.
Comments: Available
Price Range: $120.00-135.00

Name: Ruthie
Maker's Name: Horsman Doll, Inc.
Marks: HORSMAN DOLL MFG. CO., A/HORSMAN/DOLL, HORSMAN, IRENE SZOR/HORSMAN (or) Horsman Dolls, Inc.
Origin: U.S.A.
Size: 12″, 14″, 16″, 18″, 27″ & 36″
Date: circa 1959-1960s
Description: Medium brown vinyl fully jointed doll with a turning head, sculptured features, rooted black straight hair with bangs, voice box "coo" sound. Doll walks. Accessories include soap, sponge, comb, brush and mirror set, snap-lock suitcase with handle or No Accessories. All original. Excellent condition.
Comments: Available
Price Range: $75.00-90.00

Name: Softee Baby
Maker's Name: Horsman Dolls, Inc.
Marks: HORSMAN DOLL MFG. CO., A/HORSMAN/DOLL, HORSMAN, IRENE SZOR/HORSMAN (or) Horsman Dolls, Inc.
Origin: U.S.A.
Size: 10″, 12″, 13″, 14″, 16″, 18″, 20″, 22″ & 25″
Date: circa 1959-1960s
Description: Brown soft vinyl fully jointed doll with glassine brown sleep eyes, open mouth with a hole for drinking, voice box "coo" sound, sculptured toes and fingers, rooted short curly hair (black). Accessories include nursing bottle with nipple attached to wrist and/or blanket and/or suitcase, three powder puffs, soap, sponge, washcloth, funnel and/or canopy bed and/or mirror, comb, brush and rattle. All original. Excellent condition.
Comments: Available
Price Range: $75.00-90.00

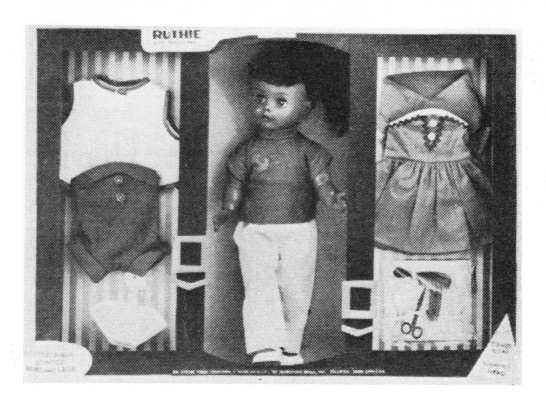

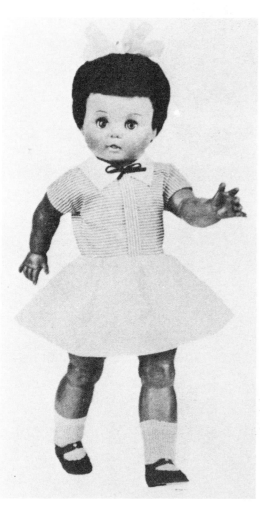

Name: Ruthie

Maker's Name: Horsman Dolls, Inc.

Marks: HORSMAN DOLL MFG. CO., A/HORSMAN/DOLL, HORSMAN, IRENE SZOR/HORSMAN (or) Horsman Dolls, Inc.

Origin: U.S.A.

Size: 13″, 15″, 17″, 19″ & 28″

Date: circa 1960

Description: Brown vinyl plastic fully jointed, tilting-turning head, rooted short black hair, sculptured features - fingers and toes. Accessories include comb, brush, mirror, soap, sponge, suitcase and/or pocketbook, beachbag, towel, sunglasses, "real" tube of "Tanfastic" suntan cream by Sea & Ski. Some dolls have No Accessories. All original. Excellent condition.

Comments: Available. *Doll with wardrobe has long straight ponytail.

Price Range: $75.00-85.00

Name: Softee Baby
Maker's Name: Horsman Dolls, Inc.
Marks: HORSMAN DOLL MFG. CO., A/HORSMAN/DOLL, HORSMAN, IRENE SZOR/HORSMAN (or) Horsman Dolls, Inc.
Origin: U.S.A.
Size: *12″, 15″, 17″, 19″, 23″, 25″ & 26″
Date: circa 1960
Description: Soft vinyl, fully jointed, medium brown color with brown glassine sleep eyes, open mouth with hole, drinks, wets, voice box "coo" sound, rooted short, curly black hair or molded tinted black hair. *Boy/girl twins or singles (single doll may have a canopy crib, blanket and pillow). All original. Excellent condition.
Comments: Available
Price Range: $50.00-75.00

Name: Ruthie Nurse
Maker's Name: Horsman Dolls, Inc.
Date: circa 1962
Price Range: $85.00-120.00
* See description for "Ruthie"

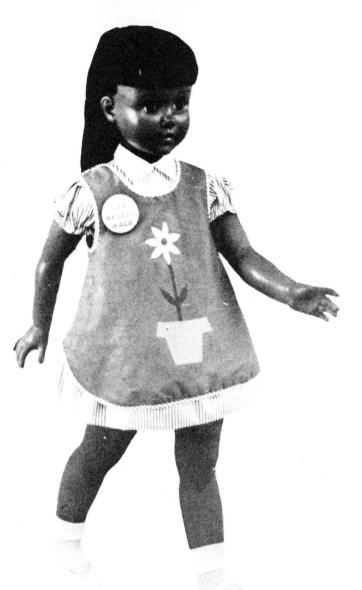

Name: Princess Peggy
Maker's Name: Horsman Dolls, Inc.
Marks: HORSMAN DOLL MFG. CO., A/HORSMAN/DOLL, HORSMAN, IRENE SZOR/HORSMAN (or) Horsman Dolls, Inc.
Origin: U.S.A.
Size: 36″
Date: circa 1960s
Description: Medium brown vinyl plastic fully jointed doll with glassine sleep eyes, closed mouth, sculptured features and toes/fingers. Rooted short curly black hair or long. All original. Excellent condition.
Comments: Available. Doll walks when led by her arm.
Price Range: $125.00-140.00

Name: Peggy Ann Bride (sub-teen)
Maker's Name: Horsman Dolls, Inc.
Marks: HORSMAN DOLL MFG. CO., A/HORSMAN/DOLL, HORSMAN, IRENE SZOR/HORSMAN (or) Horsman Dolls, Inc.
Origin: U.S.A.
Size: 12″, 15″, 17″, 19″ & 27″
Date: circa 1960
Description: Brown vinyl, glassine brown eyes, closed mouth, slim legged, fully jointed, black rooted short curled hair, floral bouquet. *Honeymoon bound suitcase with a handle, brush, mirror, comb and several outfits. Some dolls may have No Accessories. All original. Excellent condition.
Comments: Available
Price Range: $90.00-115.00

Name: Love-Me Baby
Maker's Name: Horsman Dolls, Inc.
Marks: HORSMAN DOLL MFG. CO., A/HORSMAN/DOLL, HORSMAN, IRENE SZOR/HORSMAN (or) Horsman Dolls, Inc.
Origin: U.S.A.
Size: 23″ & 26″
Date: circa 1956
Description: Brown vinyl doll with super-flex legs and arms, rooted black ponytail, voice box "coo" sound, glassine brown eyes and closed mouth. Accessories include soap, sponge, comb, brush, curlers, mirror and suitcase with a handle or No Accessories. All original. Excellent condition.
Comments: Available but not plentiful.
Price Range: $100.00-140.00

Name: Baby Precious
Maker's Name: Horsman Dolls, Inc.
Marks: HORSMAN DOLL MFG. CO., A/HORSMAN/DOLL, HORSMAN, IRENE SZOR/HORSMAN (or) Horsman Dolls, Inc.
Origin: U.S.A.
Size: 11″, 13″, 15″, 17″, 19″, 21″ & 23″
Date: circa 1957-1958
Description: Soft brown female vinyl "Fairy Skin" doll with super-flex bendable legs, turning head, voice box "coo" sound, rooted short curly black hair. All original with glassine sleep eyes and closed mouth. *Doll may be dressed as pictured or Dutch Girl / Sailor Girl / Flower Girl. Excellent condition.
Comments: Available but not plentiful.
Price Range: $125.00-150.00

Name: Walk-A-Bye
Maker's Name: Horsman Dolls, Inc.
Marks: HORSMAN DOLL MFG. CO., A/HORSMAN/DOLL, HORSMAN,
    IRENE SZOR/HORSMAN (or) Horsman Dolls, Inc.
Origin: U.S.A.
Size: 28"
Date: circa 1961
Description: Brown hard plastic, glassine brown sleep eyes, closed mouth,
    fully jointed, walks, sculptured features and hands/feet, rooted straight
    or curled long or short black hair. All original. Excellent condition.
Comments: Available
Price Range: $120.00-145.00

Name: No Name
Maker's Name: Eegee Co.
Marks: EEGEE CO. 14 BA
Origin: U.S.A.
Size: 14"
Date: © 1970
Description: Soft vinyl head, hard vinyl body. Chubby features. Negroid charateristics
    exhibiting full lips and rounded nose. Short curly hair. Brown sleep eyes. Fully
    jointed. Mouth open with a hole.
Comments: Available but not plentiful in good condition.
Courtesy of: Peggy M. Williams Collection
Price Range: $35.00-50.00

Name: Baby Buttercup
Maker's Name: Horsman Dolls, Inc.
Marks: HORSMAN DOLL MFG. CO., A/HORSMAN/DOLL, HORSMAN, IRENE SZOR/HORSMAN (or) Horsman Dolls, Inc.
Origin: U.S.A.
Size: 12″, 15″, 17″, 19″ & 22″
Date: circa 1962
Description: Brown soft vinyl, brown glassine eyes (sleep), mouth open, fully jointed, sculptured head and body, soft curved chubby arms and legs, rooted curly black hair or molded tinted black hair, voice box "coo" sound, turning head. Accessories are None or nursing bottle. All original. Excellent condition.
Comments: Available
Price Range: $55.00-75.00

Name: Teensie Tots
Maker's Name: Horsman Dolls, Inc.
Marks: HORSMAN DOLL MFG. CO., A/HORSMAN/DOLL, HORSMAN, IRENE SZOR/HORSMAN (or) Horsman Dolls, Inc.
Origin: U.S.A.
Size: 10½″
Date: circa 1962, *1st year made.
Description: Brown vinyl, fully jointed, brown glassine sleep eyes, closed mouth, rooted curly black hair with a turning head. All original. Excellent condition.
Comments: Dolls with similar features were made in 1961 but they appeared as "No Name" dolls. Black dolls of this type appeared in 1962.
Price Range: $40.00-50.00 each

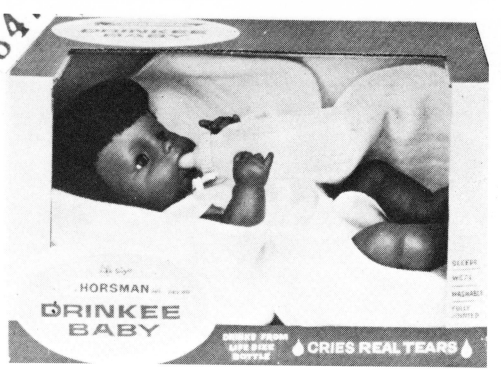

Name: Drinkee Baby
Maker's Name: Horsman Dolls, Inc.
Marks: HORSMAN DOLL MFG. CO., A/HORSMAN/DOLL, HORSMAN, IRENE SZOR/HORSMAN (or) Horsman Dolls, Inc.
Origin: U.S.A.
Size: 19″
Date: circa 1964
Description: Brown vinyl, brown glassine eyes, open mouth with a hole, fully jointed, drinks, wets and cries, sculptured head and body, turning head, soft chubby arms and legs, rooted short black hair. Full size nursing bottle with nipple. All original. Excellent condition.
Comments: *Mint and In The Box (MIB). Available.
Price Range: $45.00-60.00

Name: Thirstee Walker
Maker's Name: Horsman Dolls, Inc.
Marks: HORSMAN DOLL MFG. CO., A/HORSMAN/DOLL, HORSMAN, IRENE SZOR/HORSMAN (or) Horsman Dolls, Inc.
Origin: U.S.A.
Size: 27″
Date: circa 1965
Description: Brown vinyl, brown glassine eyes (sleep), open mouth with hole, walks, wets, cries, sculptured head and body, rooted black hair in a wispy hairstyle. Full size nursing bottle. All original. Fully jointed. Excellent condition.
Comments: Available
Price Range: $60.00-75.00

Name: "No Name" Female
Maker's Name: Unmarked
Marks: None
Origin: U.S.A.
Size: 4¼"
Date: circa 1920-1930s
Description: Celluloid female with dark brown color, fully jointed, painted features and original clothing. Excellent condition.
Comments: Available but not plentiful in the style described above. Most of the small Black celluloids are undressed or may have molded painted clothing.
Courtesy of: Angie's Doll Boutique
Price Range: $45.00-60.00

Name: Troll
Maker's Name: Denmark (no company name)
Marks: Made in Thomas Dam Denmark (enclosed in an oval)
Origin: Denmark
Size: 9½"
Date: circa 1960-1970
Description: Brown rubber character with no moveable joints, wool long brown hair, molded sculpted features with large feet and hands, brown glassine eyes. All original. Excellent condition.
Comments: Trolls were made for a short time period, approximately 15 years. The dolls were made in large quantities but many of them were discarded. Black trolls were produced in fewer quantities and thus are scarce.
Courtesy of: Angie's Doll Boutique
Price Range: $45.00-50.00

Name: "No Name" Female Toddler
Maker's Name: Japan (no company name)
Marks: JAPAN
Origin: Japan
Size: 2¼"
Date: circa 1920-1930s
Description: Brown celluloid chubby-body toddler with moveable arms, straight legs, molded painted hair and shoes, original yellow dress. Painted features. Excellent condition.
Comments: Available. Dressed styles as described above are not plentiful.
Courtesy of: Angie's Doll Boutique
Price Range: $40.00-55.00

Name: Ginny-type
Maker's Name: Unmarked
Marks: None
Origin: U.S.A.
Size: 7½"
Date: circa 1940s-1950s
Description: Hard plastic brown doll with a mohair wig, brown sleep eyes, fully jointed, original hat and clothing. Excellent condition. *Strung straight legs.
Comments: Black Ginny dolls are available but not plentiful.
Courtesy of: Angie's Doll Boutique
Price Range: $160.00-220.00

Name: Chansi
Maker's Name: Japan (no company name)
Marks: Chansi (enclosed in an oval) MADE IN JAPAN
Origin: Japan
Size: 3¾"
Date: circa 1910-1930s
Description: Brown celluloid toddler with a chubby molded body, beautiful curly molded tinted hair with a bow-notch, original ribbon, molded painted naturalistic Negroid features, fully jointed (strung). Very good condition.
Comments: A celluloid doll of the quality described above is not plentiful from JAPAN.
Courtesy of: Angie's Doll Boutique
Price Range: $30.00-45.00

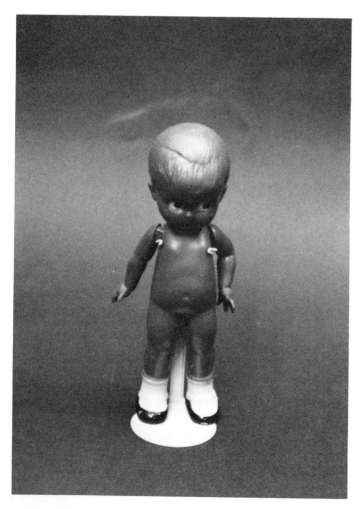

Name: "No Name" Toddler Boy
Maker's Name: Knickerbocker, Plastic Co.
Marks: Knickerbocker, Plastic Co. / Glendale, Calif.
Origin: U.S.A.
Size: 6"
Date: circa 1940s
Description: All celluloid brown toddler with jointed arms, molded painted hair, features, shoes/socks. Very good condition.
Comments: Available and plentiful.
Courtesy of: Angie's Doll Boutique
Price Range: $25.00-30.00

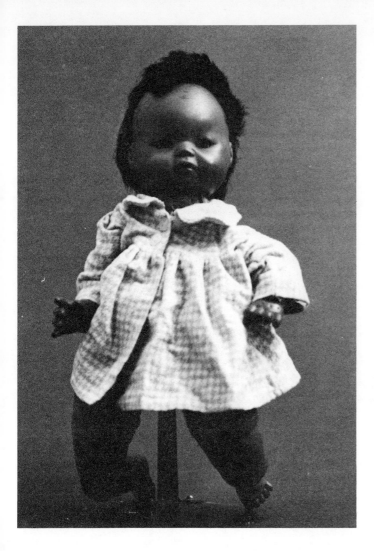

Name: "No Name" Female Body
Maker's Name: J-CEY
Marks: 12 EP J-CEY
Origin: U.S.A.
Size: 15"
Date: circa 1960s-1970
Description: Vinyl head, arms & legs with a cloth stuffed body. Negroid features, brown glassine eyes, synthetic rooted short black hair. Chubby baby features. Good condition.
Comments: Available and plentiful.
Courtesy of: Davern Collection
Price Range: $45.00-55.00

Name: "No Name" Female Girl
Maker's Name: Japan (no company name)
Marks: 62 MADE IN JAPAN (upward-swing style of letter arrangement)
Origin: Japan
Size: 5"
Date: circa 1960s
Description: Soft vinyl dark brown toddler, synthetic long black hair in a single braid, painted molded features, jointed arms. Original clothing. Very good condition.
Comments: Available.
Courtesy of: Davern Collection
Price Range: $18.00-25.00

Name: Aunt Jemima Family
Maker's Name: Unmarked
Marks: (Character's names) Uncle Mose, Aunt Jemima, Diana, Wade. *(Marked on the back except Aunt Jemima)
Origin: U.S.A.
Size: 12¼″ Adults, 8¼″ Children
Date: circa 1930-1950s
Description: Thick lithographed plastic cut-outs. Dolls were cut out and stitched/stuffed at home.
Comments: Entire families are scarce but available.
Courtesy of: Davern Collection
Price Range: $175.00-225.00 family
          60.00- 70.00 each (adults)
          45.00- 55.00 each (children)

Name: Hottentot (Black Kewpie)
Maker's Name: Oriental
Marks: Oriental (written in an upswing arrangement) Sawtooth symbol
Origin: Japan
Size: 12¾″
Date: circa 1940-1950s
Description: Early hard plastic black chubby body male doll with jointed arms, molded painted features - hair and tiny blue wings on the back of the shoulders. Excellent condition.
Comments: Available.
Courtesy of: Yesteryear's Museum
Price Range: $100.00-145.00

Name: "No Name" Male Toddlers
Maker's Name: Japan (no company name)
Marks: JAPAN
Origin: Japan
Size: (largest to smallest) 6½″, 5½″, 3⅞″, 3½″, 3″ & 2¼″
Date: circa 1920s-1930s
Description: All dark brown celluloid male dolls of varying sizes, some with jointed legs and arms, others with jointed arms only. All but one with painted molded clothing. All with painted molded hair and features. All in excellent condition.
Comments: Common and available.
Courtesy of: Davern Collection
Price Range: $18.00-40.00 (small/large)

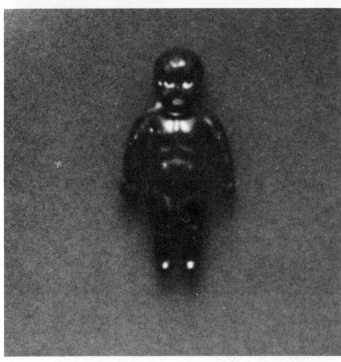

Name: Pillar Doll
Maker's Name: Unmarked
Marks: None
Origin: Germany
Size: 2″
Date: circa 1920-1930s
Description: All celluloid doll with painted features, molded well defined body. Exaggerated Negroid features. Excellent condition.
Comments: Available
Courtesy of: Yesteryear's Museum
Price Range: $25.00-35.00

Name: Watermelon Baby
Maker's Name: Unmarked
Marks: None
Origin: Germany
Size: 3″
Date: circa 1900-1920s
Description: Well made and detail Black baby of brown celluloid with jointed arms and legs, molded painted features, naturalistic Negroid features - finely detailed. Original diaper and wooden melon shaped container. Excellent condition.
Comments: Excellent example of a miniature celluloid doll in stylization although they were mass produced. Available but not plentiful in all-original condition.
Courtesy of: Yesteryear's Museum
Price Range: $80.00-100.00

Name: "No Name" Female Adult
Maker's Name: Unmarked
Marks: None
Origin: U.S.A.
Size: 8″
Date: circa 1920s-1940s
Description: Celluloid face with painted features, cloth body, original clothing and hat. Excellent condition.
Comments: Available
Courtesy of: Davern Collection
Price Range: $50.00-75.00

Name: Musicians & Market Woman
Maker's Name: Unmarked
Marks: None
Origin: Jamaica
Size: 4″ each
Date: circa 1940s-1950s
Description: Super-flex hard rubber dolls with strong molded Negroid features, eyes and mouth painted. Each figure has original clothing and instruments. Excellent condition.
Comments: Dolls came in sets of five with a female singer and also available in sets of eight, no female, and can be found as single dolls dressed in work clothing for various occupations, i.e., market lady. The dolls described are available on today's Doll Market but they are not plentiful.
Courtesy of: Davern Collection (set of four)
    Fairhaven Doll Museum (set of eight)
    Angie's Doll Boutique (single doll)
Price Range: $50.00- 75.00 (set of four) (singer missing)
    130.00-150.00 (set of eight)
    20.00- 30.00 each

Name: Dance Ballerina Dance Collection
Maker's Name: Effanbee
Marks: EFFANBEE ©1979 / 1176 (on neck), EFF & BEE (on body)
Origin: U.S.A.
Size: 11″
Date: © 1976
Description: Fully jointed vinyl plastic doll with an adult body. Black/brown straight hair in an upswept style. Medium brown sleep eyes, closed mouth and painted lips (orange-red). Well dressed.
Comment: Unplayed with condition, all original. Available but not plentiful.
Courtesy of: DeLois Sellers Collection
Price Range: $85.00-110.00

Name: Amanda / Grandes Dames
Maker's Name: Effanbee
Marks: EFFANBEE 1975/1576
Origin: U.S.A.
Size: 11″
Date: © 1975
Description: Fully jointed vinyl plastic adult body. Black/brown hair, straight and pulled back with a cascade of curled hair over the shoulders. Medium brown sleep eyes, closed mouth, painted lips. Well dressed.
Comments: Unplayed with condition, all original. Available but not plentiful.
Courtesy of: DeLois Sellers Collection
Price Range: $85.00-100.00

Name: Ruby / Grandes Dames
Maker's Name: Effanbee
Marks: EFFANBEE 1976 / 1578 (on neck)
Origin: U.S.A.
Size: 14"
Date: © 1976
Description: Fully jointed adult body. Black straight synthetic hair pulled back into a bun. Medium-brown sleep eyes. Fine features, closed mouth with painted lips. Well dressed.
Comments: Unplayed with condition, all original. Available but not plentiful.
Courtesy of: DeLois Sellers Collection
Price Range: $100.00-135.00

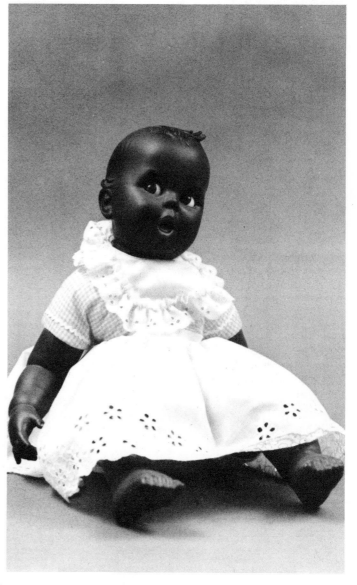

Name: Gerber Baby
Maker's Name: Gerber Productions Company
Marks: GERBER PRODUCTIONS CO. ©1979
Origin: U.S.A.
Size: 17"
Date: © 1979
Description: Fully articulated features of the face and limbs. Flirty eyes, open/closed mouth, deeply molded hair with a curled peak on top. Chubby features and body. Cotton clothing.
Comments: Unplayed with condition, all original. Available but not plentiful in unplayed with condition.
Courtesy of: DeLois Sellers Collection
Price Range: $65.00-90.00

Name: Pussy Cat
Maker's Name: Madame Alexander
Marks: ALEXANDER © 1977
Origin: U.S.A.
Size: 18″
Date: © 1977
Description: Vinyl head, arms, and legs, cloth baby's body, chubby features with closed mouth and painted lips. Medium length straight black hair, brown sleep eyes. Well dressed baby's outfit.
Comments: Unplayed with condition, all original. Available but not plentiful in the described condition.
Courtesy of: DeLois Sellers Collection
Price Range: $85.00-110.00

Name: Sweetie Pie
Maker's Name: Effanbee
Marks: EFFANBEE 1969 / 9469
Origin: U.S.A.
Size: 16″
Date: © 1969
Description: Soft vinyl head, arms, and legs, cloth chubby body. Dark brown curled hair. Brown sleep eyes. Well dressed.
Comments: Unplayed with condition, all original. Available but not plentiful.
Courtesy of: DeLois Sellers Collection
Price Range: $90.00-125.00

Name: No Name "Walking Doll"
Maker's Name: Taiwan
Marks: TAIWAN
Origin: Taiwan
Size: 26″
Date: © 1965
Description: Soft vinyl head, hard plastic fully jointed child's body (pre-teen). Long black straight hair. Brown sleep eyes. Sculptured features and body.
Comments: Played with. Doll walks when her hand is held. Available and plentiful.
Courtesy of: Peggy M. Williams Collection
Price Range: $65.00-80.00 (good condition)

Name: Chipper
Maker's Name: Effanbee
Marks: EFFANBEE 1978 / 1578
Origin: U.S.A.
Size: 14″
Date: © 1978
Description: Vinyl child's body. Fully jointed. Long straight black hair. Brown sleep eyes. Closed mouth with painted lips. Well dressed.
Comments: Unplayed with condition, all original. Available but not plentiful.
Courtesy of: DeLois Sellers Collection
Price Range: $70.00-85.00

Name: No Name
Maker's Name: Horsman Doll, Inc.
Marks: HORSMAN DOLL INC. © 1974
Origin: U.S.A.
Size: 12″
Date: © 1974
Description: Fully jointed vinyl chubby baby's doll. Short wispy black hair. Brown sleep eyes. Open/closed mouth, painted lips. Long black eye lashes.
Comments: Played with condition, all original. Available and plentiful.
Courtesy of: Peggy M. Williams Collection
Price Range: $40.00-50.00

Name: No Name
Maker's Name: Horsman Dolls Inc.
Marks: HORSMAN © 1960
Origin: U.S.A.
Date: © 1960
Description: Fully jointed chubby vinyl body. Short black curled hair. Brown sleep eyes. Open mouth with a hole. Redressed.
Comments: Played with condition. Redressed. Available and plentiful.
Courtesy of: Peggy M. Williams Collection
Price Range: $25.00-45.00

Name: No Name
Maker's Name: Horsman Dolls Inc.
Marks: HORSMAN 30-4
Origin: U.S.A.
Size: 15″
Date: © 1965-1970
Description: Fully jointed, soft vinyl head, hard vinyl body, long straight black hair. Greenish-black sleep eyes, closed mouth, painted lips. Well dressed with replaced hair accessories.
Comments: Played with. Original clothing. Available and plentiful.
Courtesy of: Peggy M. Williams Collection
Price Range: $40.00-55.00

Name: No Name
Maker's Name: Not Available
Marks: K4296
Origin: U.S.A.
Size: 15″
Date: © 1965-1970
Description: Fully jointed chubby baby's body. Soft vinyl head/hard vinyl body. Short black curled hair. Brown sleep eyes. Closed mouth with painted lips.
Comments: Played with condition. Many American and foreign doll companies used mold numbers appearing on the nape of the doll's neck in addition to their company's name. The above doll only has a mold number which makes it difficult to attribute it to any company. Older dolls prior to the 1940s can sometimes be identified by the mold numbers alone. German and French companies usually registered their mold numbers. Available and plentiful.
Courtesy of: Peggy M. Williams Collection
Price Range: $35.00-45.00

Name: No Name
Maker's Name: Eugene Doll Co.
Marks: 4035 / 13 /E3001 /715 MADE IN TAIWAN © EUGENE DOLL 1976 26
Origin: Taiwan
Size: 15″
Date: © 1976
Description: Fully jointed slim girl's body. Soft vinyl head, hard vinyl body. Bright light brown eyes/sleep. Mouth slightly open with painted full lips. Straight black long hair.
Comments: Played with condition. Slim bodied dolls are not plentiful.
Courtesy of: Peggy M. Williams Collection
Price Range: $35.00-50.00

Name: No Name
Maker's Name: Effanbee
Marks: EB 15
Origin: U.S.A.
Size: 15″
Date: © 1970
Description: Fully jointed chubby body. Soft vinyl head, hard vinyl body. Short straight curled hair. Closed mouth with painted lips. Large medium brown sleep eyes.
Comments: Played with condition. Available.
Courtesy of: Peggy M. Williams Collection
Price Range: $45.00-60.00

Name: No Name
Maker's Name: Horsman Doll Inc.
Marks: HORSMAN DOLL INC. / 6716
Origin: U.S.A.
Size: 16″
Date: © 1960-1965
Description: Vinyl plastic. Well dressed pre-teen girl with molded painted features and painted lips, brown sleep eyes. Long straight dark brown hair. All original.
Comments: Dolls like the one described above are hard to find in their original condition. Doll has molded rubber roman sandals with the original laces secured around the doll's legs.
Courtesy of: Peggy M. Williams Collection
Price Range: $85.00-100.00

Name: Saucy Walker
Maker's Name: Unmarked
Marks: None
Origin: U.S.A.
Size: 17″
Date: © 1950s
Description: Hard plastic. Rich brown coloring. Long black straight hair in two braids and bangs. Fully jointed with a walking mechanism which is activated when the doll turns her head. Brown sleep eyes, open mouth with teeth and painted lips.
Comments: Available but not plentiful in the "Black" versions. Doll is redressed but in very good condition.
Courtesy of: Peggy M. Williams Collection
Price Range: $125.00-145.00 (all original condition)
         90.00- 100.00 (good condition/redressed)

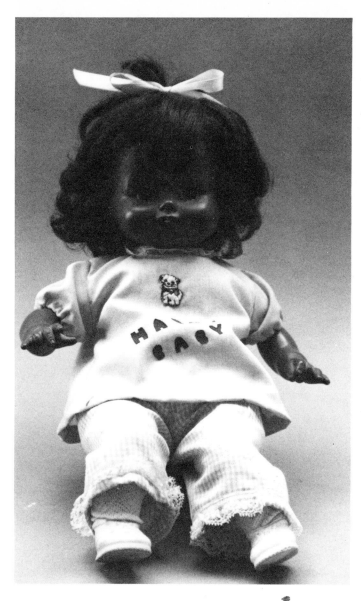

Name: Happy Baby
Maker's Name: Horsman Dolls Inc.
Marks: HORSMAN DOLLS INC. 19©70
Origin: U.S.A.
Date: © 1970
Description: Soft vinyl head, arms, legs and cloth body. Smiling baby doll with a laughing box activated by a battery operated switch. Open mouth with one tooth. Painted brown eyes. Straight dark brown short hair.
Comments: Available and plentiful.
Courtesy of: Peggy M. Williams Collection
Price Range: $40.00-55.00

Name: No Name
Maker's Name: Jolly Toys Inc., small doll by Japan
Marks: JOLLY TOYS INC.
Origin: U.S.A., Japan (small doll)
Size: 14″ (large); 5″ (small)
Date: © 1968 (both dolls)
Description: Soft vinyl head, hard plastic body, small doll has soft vinyl. Both dolls are fully jointed, they have black straight hair. The largest doll has brown sleep eyes, the smallest doll has painted eyes. Lips are painted.
Comments: Available and plentiful. The largest doll is redressed. The above dolls did not come together, they were sold separately on independent markets. Small doll is black and the largest one is medium brown.
Courtesy of: Peggy M. Williams Collection
Price Range: $30.00-45.00 (large doll)
  12.00-20.00 (small doll)

Name: No Name
Maker's Name: Not Available
Marks: E 6 15
Origin: U.S.A.
Size: 16″
Date: © 1968-1970
Description: Vinyl. Fully jointed chubby body. Straight short black hair. Brown sleep
   eyes, painted lips.
Comments: Available and plentiful.
Courtesy of: Peggy M. Williams Collection
Price Range: $25.00-40.00

Name: No Name
Maker's Name: Unmarked
Marks: None
Origin: U.S.A.
Size: 20″
Date: © 1958-1965
Description: Soft vinyl head, hard plastic body. Fully jointed slim young adult body.
   Short black curled hair, dark brown sleep eyes. High-heeled feet. Closed mouth
   with painted lips.
Comments: Available but not plentiful in good condition.
Courtesy of: Peggy M. Williams Collection
Price Range: $80.00-95.00

Name: No Name
Maker's Name: Effanbee
Marks: EFFANBEE
Origin: U.S.A.
Size: 12″
Date: © 1970s
Description: Vinyl. Slim young adult body. Brown curled short hair. Dark brown sleep
  eyes. Puckered lips painted red and closed. Fully jointed. Well dressed.
Comments: Available but not plentiful.
Courtesy of: Peggy M. Williams Collection
Price Range: $70.00-90.00

Name: No Name
Maker's Name: Hong Kong
Marks: HONG KONG
Origin: Hong Kong
Size: 12″
Date: © 1970
Description: Soft vinyl head, hard vinyl body. Light brown slim girl's body. Straight
  black long hair with bangs. Fully jointed. Closed mouth with full unpainted lips.
Comments: Available and plentiful.
Courtesy of: Peggy M. Williams Collection
Price Range: $25.00-35.00

Name: No Name
Maker's Name: Eegee Co.
Marks: EEGEE CO. 14 BA
Origin: U.S.A.
Size: 14″
Date: © 1970
Description: Soft vinyl head, hard vinyl body. Chubby features. Negroid charateristics exhibiting full lips and rounded nose. Short curly hair. Brown sleep eyes. Fully jointed. Mouth open with a hole.
Comments: Available but not plentiful in good condition.
Courtesy of: Peggy M. Williams Collection
Price Range: $30.00-45.00

Name: No Name
Maker's Name: Horsman Dolls Inc.
Marks: HORSMAN DOLLS INC. 67151
Origin: U.S.A.
Size: 14″
Date: © 1965
Description: Soft vinyl head, hard vinyl body. Chubby fully jointed body. Smiling face, open mouth with a hole. Short straight black hair. Dark brown sleep eyes.
Comments: Available and plentiful.
Courtesy of: Peggy M. Williams Collection
Price Range: $30.00-45.00

Name: No Name
Maker's Name: Sharing
Marks: SHARING NO. 3001 MADE IN HONG KONG
Origin: Hong Kong
Size: 14½″
Date: © 1965-1970
Description: Vinyl. Fully jointed adult slim body. Short curled black hair. High-heeled feet. Black painted eyes with blue eye shadow. Painted closed lips.
Comments: Available but not plentiful in good condition.
Courtesy of: Peggy M. Williams Collection
Price Range: $30.00-45.00

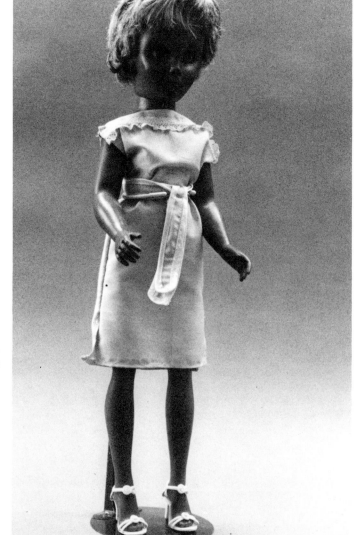

Name: No Name
Maker's Name: Unmarked
Marks: None
Origin: U.S.A.
Size: 19″
Date: © 1965-1970
Description: Soft vinyl head, vinyl plastic body. Fully jointed adult body. Salt and pepper hair (black and gray), short and curled. Honey-brown sleep eyes. Closed mouth with painted lips. High-heeled feet.
Comments: Available but not plentiful.
Courtesy of: Peggy M. Williams Collection
Price Range: $50.00-65.00

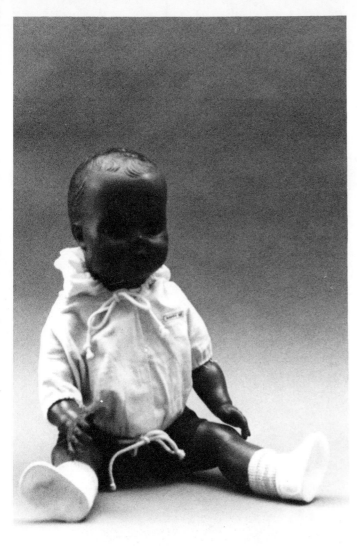

Name: No Name
Maker's Name: Not Available
Marks: A E 578 31
Origin: U.S.A.
Size: 19"
Date: © 1950s
Description: Soft vinyl and hard plastic body. Fully jointed chubby bodied boy. Molded black tinted hair. Large brown sleep eyes. Negroid features with an open mouth and hole.
Comments: Available but not plentiful. Male dolls are scarce and Black male dolls are highly sought after when well made.
Courtesy of: Peggy M. Williams Collection
Price Range: $60.00-75.00

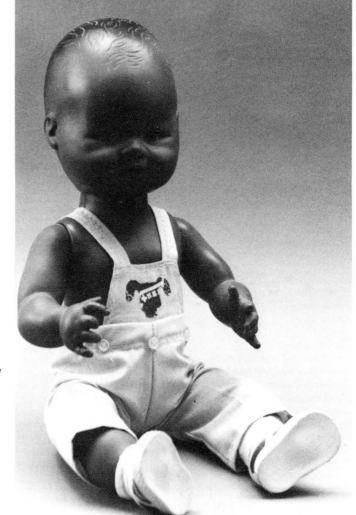

Name: No Name
Maker's Name: Plated Moulds Inc.
Marks: PLATED MOULDS INC.
Origin: U.S.A.
Size: 16"
Date: © 1961
Description: Vinyl head, hard plastic body. Fully jointed chubby bodied boy. Stationary brown eyes. Molded tinted black hair. Open mouth with a hole, painted lips.
Comments: Available and plentiful. Redressed, good condition.
Courtesy of: Peggy M. Williams Collection
Price Range: $25.00-35.00

Name: No Name
Maker's Name: Horsman Dolls Inc.
Marks: HORSMAN DOLLS INC 1964 BC 161
Origin: U.S.A.
Size: 15"
Date: © 1964
Description: Soft vinyl. Fully jointed. Short black curly hair. Brown sleep eyes. Open mouth with a hole. Chubby features.
Comments: Available but not plentiful in good condition.
Courtesy of: Peggy M. Williams Collection
Price Range: $40.00-55.00

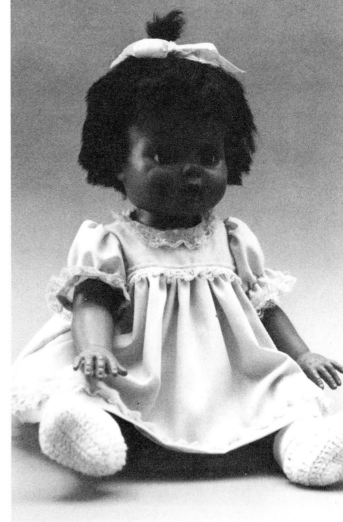

Name: No Name
Maker's Name: Not Available
Marks: A E 478 22
Origin: U.S.A.
Size: 17"
Date: © 1965-68
Description: Soft vinyl. Fully jointed chubby body. Short black straight hair. Open mouth with a hole. Large dark brown sleep eyes. Well dressed.
Comments: Available but not plentiful in good condition.
Courtesy of: Peggy M. Williams Collection
Price Range: $30.00-45.00

Name: Christie
Maker's Name: Ideal Toy Corp
Marks: 1972 IDEAL TOY CORP. GHB - H - 235
Origin: U.S.A.
Size: 22″
Date: © 1972
Description: Soft vinyl. Large chubby body. Dark brown color. Smiling expression with
    teeth showing. Negroid features. Stationary dark brown eyes. Long black straight
    hair.
Comments: Available. Doll above is redressed and in very good condition.
Courtesy of: Peggy M. Williams Collection
Price Range: $75.00-85.00 (as is - redressed)
            100.00-110.00 (all original / good condition)

Name: No Name
Maker's Name: Taiwan
Marks: TAIWAN
Origin: Taiwan
Size: 22″
Date: © 1960-1968
Description: Vinyl head, plastic body. Fully jointed. Long black straight hair. Closed
    mouth with painted lips. Brown sleep eyes. All original.
Comments: Available but not plentiful in all-original outfit as seen above.
Courtesy of: Peggy M. Williams Collection
Price Range: $45.00-65.00

Name: No Name
Maker's Name: Taiwan
Marks: MADE IN TAIWAN
Origin: Taiwan
Size: 22"
Date: © 1968
Description: Vinyl head, plastic body. Fully jointed girl's body, long straight black hair, dark brown eyes, closed mouth with painted lips.
Comments: Available.
Courtesy of: Peggy M. Williams Collection
Price Range: $40.00-50.00

Name: No Name
Maker's Name: Unmarked
Marks: None
Origin: U.S.A.
Size: 24"
Date: © 1968-1970
Description: Vinyl plastic. Fully jointed girl's body. Honey brown sleep eyes. Closed mouth with painted lips. Long straight black hair.
Comments: Available. Redressed.
Courtesy of: Peggy M. Williams Collection
Price Range: $40.00-50.00

Name: No Name
Maker's Name: Unmarked
Marks: None
Origin: U.S.A.
Size: 23″
Date: © 1968-1972
Description: Vinyl plastic. Fully jointed. Closed mouth with painted lips. Curly Afro wig (medium black/brown color). Brown sleep eyes.
Comments: Available and plentiful.
Courtesy of: Peggy M. Williams Collection
Price Range: $40.00-50.00

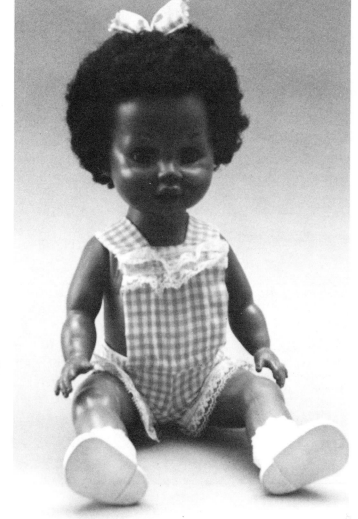

Name: No Name
Maker's Name: Jolly Toys, Inc.
Marks: JOLLY TOYS, INC. 19 © 66 8
Origin: U.S.A.
Size: 13½″
Date: © 1966
Description: Vinyl. Fully jointed chubby features. Negroid characteristics exhibiting full lips and broad nose. Mouth open with a hole. Large brown eyes. Short curly Afro style hair.
Comments: Available but not plentiful in good condition.
Courtesy of: Peggy M. Williams Collection
Price Range: $45.00-55.00

Name: No Name
Maker's Name: Shindana Toys
Marks: SHINDANA TOYS 1972
Origin: U.S.A.
Size: 11½″
Date: © 1972
Description: Vinyl. Fully jointed chubby body with Negroid features. Brown eyes (stationary). Open mouth with a hole. Hair curly and black.
Comments: Available but not plentiful in good condition. Many dolls made by the above company were destroyed by children at play. The Shindana Company became defunct several years ago, thus making the dolls, even scarcer on the collectibles market.
Courtesy of: Peggy M. Williams Collection
Price Range: $40.00-55.00

Name: No Name
Maker's Name: Eugene Doll Company
Marks: E 7020 / MADE IN TAIWAN / © EUGENE DOLL
Origin: Taiwan
Size: 25″
Date: © 1977
Description: Soft vinyl head, plastic body. Fully jointed. Long curled black hair. Brown sleep eyes. Closed mouth with painted lips (puckered lips).
Comments: Available.
Courtesy of: Peggy M. Williams Collection
Price Range: $45.00-55.00

Name: Barbie Family "Malibu Christie" / "Live Action Christie"
Maker's Name: Mattel, Inc.
Marks: © MATTEL, INC. 1966 TAIWAN
Origin: Taiwan
Size: 12″
Date: © 1970s
Description: Vinyl plastic. Fully jointed, ball jointed arms, twisting waist. Adult slim body with high heeled feet. Long black full bodied hair. Brown eyes.
Comments: Available but not plentiful in good condition. Arms posed at the elbows.
Courtesy of: La Shawne Highs Collection
Price Range: $40.00-55.00 (played with good condition)
          110.00-125.00 (mint to very good unplayed with condition)

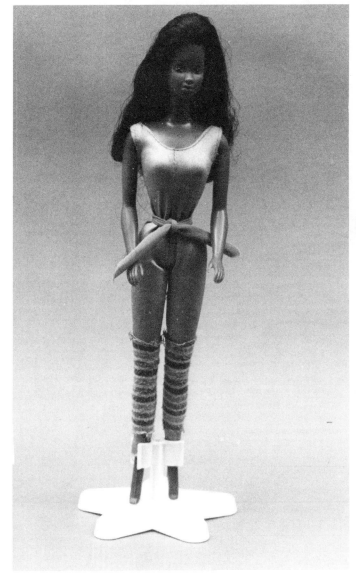

Name: Barbie Family "Mailbu Christie" / "Live Action Christie"
Maker's Name: Mattel, Inc.
Marks: MATTTEL, INC. 1966 PHILIPPINES
Origin: Philippines
Size: 12″
Date: © 1970s
Description: Vinyl plastic. Fully jointed young adult body. Full lips and painted eyes. Long full bodied black hair. High-heeled feet. Twisting waist.
Comments: Available but not plentiful in good condition.
Courtesy of: La Shawne Highs Collection
Price Range: $40.00-55.00 (played with good condition)
          110.00-125.00 (mint to very good condition, unplayed with)

Name: Barbie Family "Malibu Christie" / "Live Action Christie"
Maker's Name: Mattel, Inc.
Marks: © MATTEL, INC. 1966 TAIWAN (on lower back)
Origin: Taiwan
Size: 12"
Date: © 1970s
Description: Vinyl plastic. Fully jointed, ball jointed arms, oxidized red hair, brown painted eyes, slim young adult body, high-heeled feet. Full lips painted and closed. Twisting waist.
Comments: Available but not plentiful in good condition. Arms posed at the elbows. Oxidized hair will increase the price.
Courtesy of: La Shawne Highs Collection
Price Range: $40.00-55.00 (played with good condition)
110.00-125.00 (mint to very good condition, unplayed with)

Name: Barbie Family "Malibu Christie" / "Live Action Christie"
Maker's Name: Mattel, Inc.
Marks: MATTEL, INC. 1966 PHILIPPINES
Origin: Philippines
Size: 12"
Date: © 1970s
Description: Vinyl plastic. Fully jointed, slim young adult body, painted brown eyes. Closed mouth with full lips painted. Long full bodied brown hair. High-heeled feet. Twisting waist.
Comments: Available but not plentiful in good condition.
Courtesy of: La Shawne Highs Collection
Price Range: $40.00-55.00 (played with, good condition)
110.00-125.00 (mint to very good, unplayed with condition)

Name: Bride Doll
Maker's Name: Taiwan
Marks: TAIWAN © 1968
Origin: Taiwan
Size: 12″
Date: © 1968
Description: Vinyl and thin soft plastic. Fully jointed, slim young adult body, high-heeled feet, black short curled hair, open mouth with teeth showing. Twisting waist.
Comments: Available and plentiful.
Courtesy of: La Shawne Highs Collection
Price Range: $20.00-30.00
    40.00-50.00 with twisting waist
The above prices reflect dolls in very good to mint condition.

Name: No Name
Maker's Name: Not Available
Marks: 8
Origin: U.S.A.
Size: 20″
Date: © 1968-1972
Description: Hard vinyl head, plastic body. Fully jointed, brown sleep eyes, orange short curled hair. Chubby child's body.
Comments: Available.
Price Range: $25.00-40.00

Name: Lester
Maker's Name: Eegee Company
Marks: 1978 LESTER © EEGEE CO 24
Origin: U.S.A.
Size: 24″
Date: © 1978
Description: Hard vinyl head and arms, cloth body and legs. Male ventriloquist doll from the "Black" Willie Tyler and Lester (doll) duo. Black painted eyes, short black curly hair. Lower lip opens by pulling the cord on the doll's neck.
Comments: Available.
Courtesy of: La Shawne Highs Collection
Price Range: $45.00-55.00 (mint to very good condition)

Name: No Name
Maker's Name: Uneeda Doll Comany
Marks: 3178 ME © UNEEDA DOLL CO. INC. MCMLXXVI
Origin: U.S.A.
Size: 31″
Date: © 1976
Description: Hard plastic. Fully jointed, brown sleep eyes, closed mouth with painted lips, long black straight hair (upswept style).
Comments: Available. Redressed and in good condition.
Courtesy of: La Shawne Highs Collection
Price Range: $65.00-90.00

Name: No Name
Maker's Name: Unmarked
Marks: None
Origin: U.S.A.
Size: 22″
Date: © 1968-1975
Description: Hard plastic. Fully jointed. Light brown sleep eyes, closed mouth with tinted lips. Short Afro hair style.
Comments: Available but not plentiful in good condition.
Courtesy of: La Shawne Highs Collection
Price Range: $55.00-75.00

Name: No Name
Maker's Name: Unmarked
Marks: None
Origin: U.S.A.
Size: 32″
Date: © 1970-1976
Description: Hard plastic. Fully jointed, brown sleep eyes, black hair, closed mouth with painted lips.
Comments: Available.
Courtesy of: La Shawne Highs Collection
Price Range: $55.00-75.00

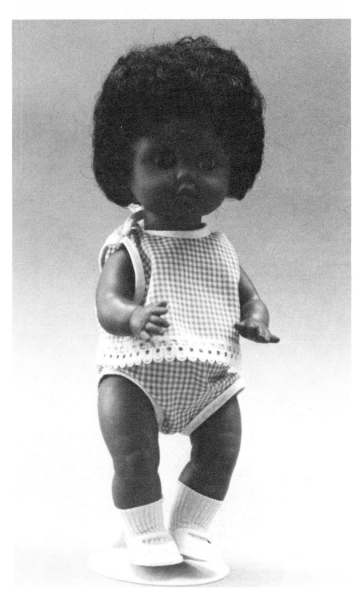

Name: No Name
Maker's Name: Shindana Toys
Marks: SHINDANA © 1975 TOYS
Origin: U.S.A.
Size: 10″
Date: © 1975
Description: Soft vinyl head, hard vinyl body. Fully jointed chubby body. Negroid features. Full lips of a flesh-brown tone. Curly black short hair. Large brown sleep eyes. Mouth slightly open.
Comments: Available but not plentiful in good condition as seen above. All original.
Courtesy of: Peggy M. Williams Collection
Price Range: $45.00-55.00 (mint to very good condition)

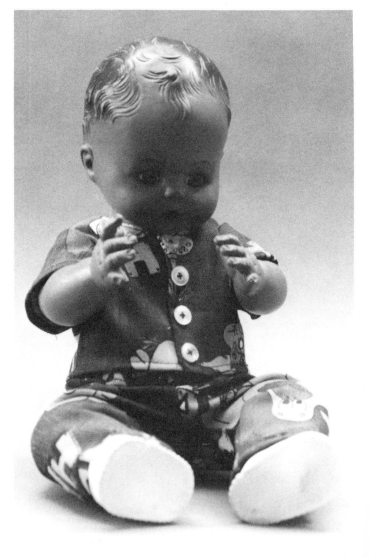

Name: No Name
Maker's Name: Effanbee
Marks: 14 EFFANBEE 19 © 68 2500
Origin: U.S.A.
Size: 14″
Date: © 1968
Description: Vinyl plastic. Fully jointed with chubby body. Large brown sleep eyes. Deeply molded black tinted hair. Open mouth with a hole and painted reddish/brown lips. All original.
Comments: Available but not plentiful in good condition.
Courtesy of: Peggy M. Williams Collection
Price Range: $50.00-65.00

Name: No Name
Maker's Name: Shindana Toys
Marks: SHINDANA © 1975 TOYS
Origin: U.S.A.
Size: 10″
Date: © 1975
Description: Soft vinyl head, hard vinyl body. Fully jointed, chubby body. Negroid features. Puckered full lips tinted flesh tone (brown). Brown sleep eyes. Long straight black hair. All original.
Comments: Available but not plentiful in the above good condition and all original.
Courtesy of: Peggy M. Williams Collection
Price Range: $45.00-55.00 (mint to very good condition)

Name: No Name
Maker's Name: Plated Moulds Inc.
Marks: PLATED MOULDS INC © 1971
Origin: U.S.A.
Size: 13″
Date: © 1971
Description: Soft vinyl head, hard vinyl body. Fully jointed, chubby body. Negroid features, open mouth with a hole. Brown sleep eyes. Short straight black hair. Original outfit.
Comments: Available but not plentiful in good condition or with synthetic hair. Most dolls by the above compnay have molded hair.
Courtesy of: Peggy M. Williams Collection
Price Range: $25.00-35.00
*Dolls with hair made by the above company are priced higher than those with molded hair.

Name: No Name
Maker's Name: Unmarked
Marks: None
Origin: U.S.A.
Size: 13"
Date: © 1965 - 1968
Description: Vinyl plastic. Fully jointed child's body. Negroid features. Open mouth with a hole and tinted flesh-tone lips (brown). Black short curly hair. Brown sleep eyes. Barrettes added to the hair, original dress.
Comments: Available.
Courtesy of: Peggy M. Williams Collection
Price Range: $30.00-45.00

Name: No Name
Maker's Name: Lorrie Doll Inc.
Marks: LORRIE DOLL INC.
Origin: U.S.A.
Size: 14"
Date: © 1968
Description: Vinyl plastic. Fully jointed chubby body. Black short curly hair. Brown sleep eyes, open mouth with a hole and full flesh tone lips. Barrettes added to the hair.
Comments: Available but not plentiful in good condition.
Courtesy of: Peggy M. Williams Collection
Price Range: $45.00-55.00

Name: No Name
Maker's Name: Reliable
Marks: RELIABLE
Origin: U.S.A.
Size: 11″
Date: © 1960s
Description: Soft vinyl head, hard vinyl body. Fully jointed stubby child's body. Impish smile with lips curled and small portion of the tongue exposed. Large painted brown eyes with high arched brows. Long straight black hair in two braids. All original with added barrettes to the hair.
Comments: Available.
Courtesy of: Peggy M. Williams Collection
Price Range: $25.00-35.00

Name: No Name
Maker's Name: Unmarked
Marks: None
Origin: Taiwan
Size: 22″
Date: © 1968-1976
Description: Soft vinyl head, legs, hard plastic with vinyl plastic body and arms. Rooted long black straight hair. Closed mouth with painted lips. Large brown sleep eyes. Redressed. Good condition.
Comments: Available.
Courtesy of: Peggy M. Williams Collection
Price Range: $50.00-65.00

Name: Sweet Tender Touch
Maker's Name: Playmate
Marks: None (except on the original box) or PLAYMATE (on neck)
Origin: U.S.A.
Size: 11½″
Date: © 1966
Description: Soft vinyl head, legs, arms and foam stuffed cloth body. Cuddly soft brown baby's body with Negroid features. Puckered lips tinted flesh tone (brown) with

a hole. Large brown sleep eyes. Short straight black hair. Doll holds a tiny 2″ vinyl head doll with a foam stuffed body, painted features with Negroid characteristics. All original.
Comments: Available but not in mint condition as above or rarely found in good unplayed with condition.
Courtesy of: DeLois Sellers Collection
Price Range: $50.00-60.00 (mint to very good condition)

Name: No-Name
Maker's Name: Beatrice Wright
Marks: Beatrice Wright
Origin: U.S.A.
Size: 18″
Date: circa 1967
Description: Hard plastic, dark brown doll with synthetic hair (rooted). Redressed. Excellent condition.
Comments: Common but not plentiful.
Courtesy of: Village Antiques, Inc., Tampa, Florida
Price Range: $65.00-90.00 (excellent condition and/or all original good condition)

Name: No Name
Maker's Name: Not Available
Marks: K8
Origin: U.S.A.
Size: 15″
Date: © 1970
Description: Fully jointed slim pre-teen girls' body. Soft vinyl head, hard vinyl body. Curly short black hair. Large brown sleep eyes. Closed mouth with painted lips.
Comments: Available and plentiful.
Courtesy of: Peggy M. Williams' Collection
Price Range: $35.00-50.00

Name: No Name
Maker's Name: P.M. Sales Inc.
Marks: AE 6 P.M. SALES INC.
Origin: U.S.A.
Size: 19½″
Date: © 1968-1970
Description: Bronze color fully jointed teenage girl with a developed female body. Soft vinyl head and hard vinyl body. Reddish brown long layered cut hair. Chestnut brown large eyes (sleep). Closed mouth with painted lips.
Comments: Available but not plentiful in good condition.
Courtesy of: Peggy M. Williams' Collection
Price Range: $55.00-65.00

Bisque Dolls

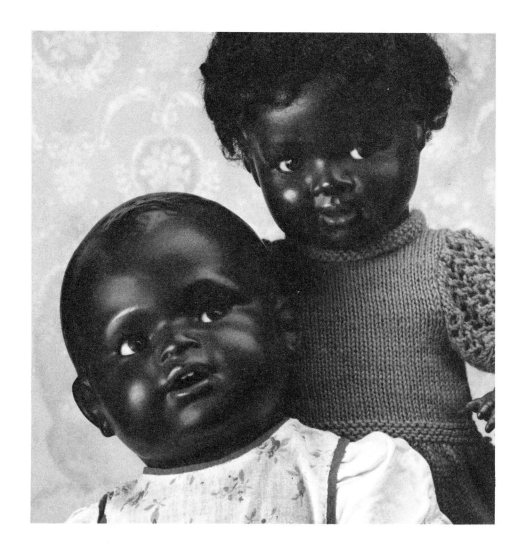

Name: Rosebud
Maker's Name: Unmarked
Marks: Rosebud (on head)
Origin: Germany
Size: 16″
Date: circa 1890-1920s
Description: Brown bisque head with stationary glass eyes, jointed at neck and shoulders. Cloth body, all original clothing. Lower extremities made of bisque. Excellent condition.
Comments: Scarce but available.
Courtesy of: Silver Springs "Museum"
Price Range: $300.00-400.00

Name: "No Name" Female Adult
Maker's Name: Germany (no company name)
Marks: Germany (in script)
Origin: Germany
Size: 9″
Date: circa 1900-1920s
Description: Soft brown bisque socket head with black glass stationary eyes, black mohair wig, fully jointed light brown composition body, open mouth with teeth, red lips, stroked eye brows. Original Jamaican outfit. Excellent condition.
Comments: Available but not plentiful.
Courtesy of: Silver Springs "Museum"
Price Range: $250.00-350.00

Name: "No Name"
Maker's Name: Unmarked
Marks: None
Origin: Germany
Size: 10½″
Date: circa 1900-1920s
Description: Brown bisque head (socket) with a fully jointed brown papier mache body. Glass black stationary eyes, painted lips with fat facial cheeks. Dark reddish brown human hair short wig. All original. Entire outfit knitted (hat, socks, dress and bloomers). Excellent condition.
Comments: Available but not plentiful.
Courtesy of: Silver Springs "Museum"
Price Range: $200.00-275.00

Name: "No Name"
Maker's Name: Unmarked
Marks: None
Origin: U.S.A.
Size: 4"
Date: circa 1900-1910
Description: All bisque brown jointed doll with painted dark brown eyes, tinted Black baby fine hair, open mouth with Negroid features. Original felt diaper and soft fleece blanket. Excellent condition.
Comments: Available but not plentiful. American-made dolls of this type were made in Japan but the features were exaggerated. Germany and France made tiny naturalistic Black dolls but "very few" were made in the U.S.A.
Courtesy of: Silver Springs "Museum"
Price Range: $65.00-85.00

Name: "No Name"
Maker's Name: Unmarked
Marks: None
Origin: Japan
Size: 4⅜"
Date: circa 1920s
Description: Black-brown bisque girl doll with molded painted features, three tufts of human hair espouting from the head. All original. Excellent condition.
Comments: Available and plentiful.
Courtesy of: Silver Springs "Museum"
Price Range: $45.00-60.00

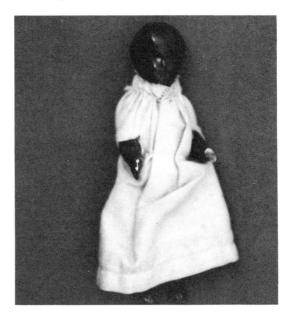

Name: "No Name" Female Girl
Maker's Name: Unmarked
Marks: None
Origin: Germany
Size: 5⅜"
Date: circa 1890s-1920s
Description: Dark brown bisque head with finely detailed features, glass brown stationary eyes, fully jointed at the shoulders, elbows, hips, knees, wrists and socket head, open mouth with teeth. All original clothing, black human hair wig. Excellent condition.

Comments: Scarce
Courtesy of: Silver Springs "Museum"
Price Range: $275.00-375.00

Name: Frozen Charlotte
Maker's Name: Unmarked
Marks: None
Origin: U.S.A.
Size: 3½"
Date: circa 1870s-1890s
Description: China black adult, molded painted features. Well articulated fingers and toes. Molded 19th century hair style with a part in the middle. Original muslin underskirt. Chubby body. Very good condition.
Comments: Black Chinas are available but scarce when they are dressed in original clothing (or any clothing) and finely detailed features as the doll described above.
Price Range: $175.00-250.00

Name: "No Name"
Maker's Name: Unmarked
Marks: 34-17
Origin: Germany
Size: 8″
Date: circa 1900-1920s
Description: Brown bisque socket head on a composition body. Glass stationary eyes, fully jointed, molded chubby features. Leather boots and original clothing. Doll holds a White small baby made of 1-piece composition. Excellent condition.
Comments: Available. *Crude composition body.
Courtesy of: Dolly Wares Doll Museum
Price Range: $275.00-325.00

Name: Wiseman
Maker's Name: Italy (no company name)
Marks: None
Origin: Italy
Size: 14″
Date: circa 1750-1800
Description: Terra Cotta head with molded exquisitely detailed features, curly molded tinted hair and inset glass eyes. Wooden carved body. Finely dressed. Articulated hands and molded feet (no details). Legs and ears adorned with jewelry. All original and in excellent condition. Fully jointed.
Comments: Rare
Courtesy of: Dolly Wares Doll Museum
Price Range: $450.00-600.00

Name: Kewpie (Hottentot)
Maker's Name: Germany (no company name)
Marks: Germany
Origin: Germany
Size: 6″
Date: circa 1920s
Description: Black and White bisque dolls came as a pair. The Black doll has a black color finish with rubbed-oil gloss. Moveable arms, stationary legs, side glancing painted eyes. All original with original lithographed box. Kewpie heart-shaped label on the chest of the White doll. Excellent condition.
Comments: Available but scarce in the above all original condition.
Courtesy of: Dolly Wares Doll Museum
Price Range: $550.00-650.00 pair

Name: Carribean Dancer
Maker's Name: Dara (Hattie Spiegl)
Marks: None
Origin: U.S.A.
Size: 17″
Date: circa 1960-1962
Description: Delicate chocolate colored bisque head, legs and arms with a shapely adult female body. Pierced ears with gold circle earrings, finely sculptured features and molded tinted hair. Well dressed with handmade jewelry on arms and neck. Excellent condition.
Comments: Artist doll. Rare, possibly one-of-a-kind.
Courtesy of: Doly Wares Doll Museum
Price Range: ***Too few examples***

Name: "No Name" Female Baby
Maker's Name: Japan (no company name)
Marks: JAPAN
Origin: Japan
Size: 6½"
Date: circa 1900-1920s
Description: All dark brown bisque chubby body doll with molded painted hair, unique molded braided hair and barrettes. Original skirt (satin). Good condition.
Comments: Plentiful. Clothes and hairstyles may vary.
Courtesy of: Angie's Doll Boutique
Price Range: $45.00-60.00

Name: Dream Baby
Maker's Name: Armand Marseille
Marks: AM Germany
Origin: Germany
Size: 10"
Date: circa 1925
Description: Solid domed brown bisque head with flanged neck, tiny brown glass sleep eyes, black painted hair and brows, accent dots at eye corners and nostrils, closed mouth with pouty downcast lips, brown complexion hands and lower legs. Excellent condition.
Comments: Doll has a rich brown complexion.
Courtesy of: Theriaults
Price Range: $650.00-800.00

Information for non-black dolls not available.

Name: Wonder Baby
Maker's Name: Georgene Haverrill Company
Marks: Germany 1400
Origin: Germany
Size: 13″
Date: circa 1900-1922
Description: Black bisque socket head with flanged neck and solid dome, painted black hair, tiny brown glass sleep eyes, painted accent dots at eye corners and nostrils, closed mouth, black muslin body with composition black hands, well dressed in original red and white striped baby gown. Excellent condition.
Comments: The doll was reputed to have been made by the Georgene Haverrill Company in 1922 for the Broadway musical "Tangerine" and was sold in the lobby as a promotional doll, the "Wonder Baby". Rare doll.
Courtesy of: Theriaults
Price Range: $550.00-750.00

Information for non-black dolls not available.

Name: "No Name" Female Girl (at right)
Maker's Name: Kestner
Marks: (7) on the head
Origin: Germany
Size: 12″
Date: circa 1885
Description: Brown bisque socket head, brown glass inset eyes, black painted lashes with incised eyeliner, thick
    brushstroked brows with feathered highlights, accented sculpted nostrils, closed mouth with pale shaded and
    accented lips, pierced ears, black mohair wig, brown composition and wooden ball jointed body with unjointed
    wrists. Excellent condition.
Comments: Rarity factors include soft brown complexion, closed mouth and petite size with all original body finish.
    Available but scarce.
Courtesy of: Theriaults
Price Range: $1,400.00-1,800.00

Information for non-black dolls not available.

Name: "No Name" Female Girl
Maker's Name: Simon and Halbig
Marks: S & H 1079 DEP Germany II
Origin: U.S.A.
Size: " 26"
Date: circa 1900
Description: Girl, brown bisque socket head, brown inset eyes, painted dark curled lashes, incised eyeliner, widely arched black brows with featured highlights, accent dots at each corner and sculptured nostrils, open mouth, four upper teeth, pierced ears, dark brown human hair wig, brown composition and wooden ball jointed body. Good coloring. Excellent condition.
Comments: Available but not plentiful.
Courtesy of: Theriaults
Price Range: $850.00-1,000.00

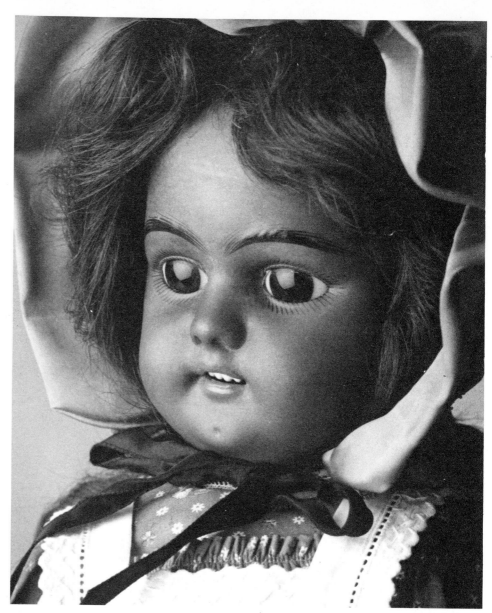

Name: "No Name" Female Girl
Maker's Name: Attributed to Simon Halbig
Marks: None
Origin: Germany
Size: 5½"
Date: circa 1885
Description: Brown bisque swivel head, dark brown glass inset eyes, black painted lashes, thick brush stroked black brows, accented nostrils, open mouth, four tiny teeth, remnants of black mohair wig, all brown bisque jointed body with molded bare feet, original clothing with a paisley shawl. Excellent condition.
Comments: Rare. Swivel head and molded bare feet are contributors to the rarity of this tiny, well defined, doll of an evenly blended brown color.
Courtesy of: Theriaults
Price Range: $750.00-950.00

Name: "No Name" Female Girl
Maker's Name: Societe Francaise de Bebe et Jouets
Marks: Unis France 71 142 60
Origin: France
Size: 11"
Date: circa 1915
Description: Brown bisque socket head, black glass pupilless inset eyes, painted lashes, accent dots at nostrils, open mouth, four teeth, black mohair wig, five piece brown papier-mache body with well detailed curled fingers. All original red gabardine fitted dress with black and white silk sash, collar and cuffs with matching cap. Excellent condition.
Comments: S.F.B.J. was formed in France in an attempt to compete with the German doll market. Doll companies of France banded together in this attempt.
Courtesy of: Theriaults
Price Range: $500.00-700.00

Name: "No Name" Female Girl
Maker's Name: Unnamed
Marks: #(3)
Origin: Germany
Size: 17"
Date: circa 1890
Description: Black bisque socket head, brown glass inset eyes, lightly painted lashes, incised eyeliner, arched brows, accent dots at eye corners and nostrils, open mouth, shaded lips, six teeth, pierced ears, black fleece wig, black composition and wooden jointed body. Excellent condition.
Comments: Fine ebony black composition with dewy patina enhances this early doll wearing original bangle earrings.
Courtesy of: Theriaults
Price Range: $650.00-850.00

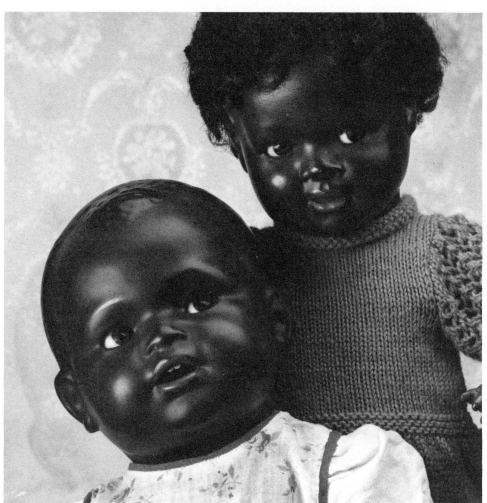

(Left Doll)
Name: "No Name" Female Baby
Maker's Name: Kammer & Reinhardt
Marks: K & R Germany
Origin: Germany
Size: 20"
Date: circa 1925
Description: Solid domed flanged head of hard terra cotta-blend material has rich dark brown complexion, sculpted and painted tightly curled black baby hair, black brows, brown glass sleep and flirty eyes, accented nostrils, open mouth with richly shaded red lips, two upper teeth, brown muslin torso, composition arms with curled fingers and two realistically outstretched fingers, brown composition bent limb baby legs, well dressed.
Comments: Rare model with strong Negroid features.
Courtesy of: Theriaults
Price Range: $700.00-950.00

(Right Doll)
Name: "No Name" Female Girl
Maker's Name: Attributed to "Konig and Warneck"
Marks: 134/12
Origin: Germany
Size: 18"
Date: circa 1925
Description: Hard terra cotta-blend socket head with rick brown complexion, brown glass sleep and flirty eyes, real lashes, accented nostrils, boldly shaped nose, open/closed mouth with molded upper teeth, richly shaded lips, black fleeced curly hair, five piece brown composition body. Excellent condition.
Comments: Doll has a mischievous look with a slightly smiling expression. The realistic Negroid features is enhanced by the rich brown complexion. Scarce.
Price Range: $700.00-850.00

Name: "No Name" African Baby
Maker's Name: Heubach Koppelsdorf
Marks: Heubach Koppelsdorf
Origin: Germany
Size: 10½"
Date: circa 1920
Description: Solid domed ebony black bisque socket head, brown glass inset side glancing eyes, black painted lashes, tuft of black wiry (animal?) hair at the top of the head, incised breather nostrils, wide row of teeth in open/closed mouth, pierced ears and nose, original black papier-mache five piece bent limb body. Excellent condition.
Comments: Exaggerated features. Scarce.
Courtesy of: Theriaults
Price Range: $650.00-850.00

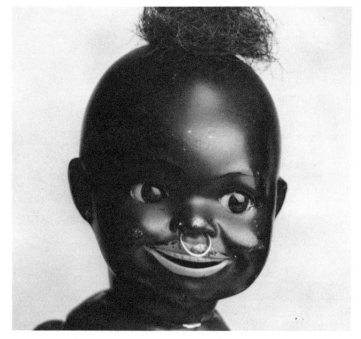

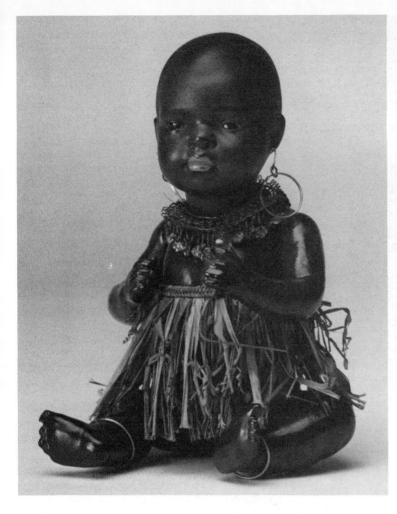

Name: "No Name" African Baby girl
Maker's Name: Heubach Kopplesdorf
Marks: Heubach Kopplesdorf 399 10/0 DRGM Germany
Origin: Germany
Size: 10"
Date: circa 1910
Description: Solid domed brown bisque socket head, painted black baby hair and brows, tiny brown glass inset eyes, painted lashes, closed mouth with fully rich lips, pierced ears with original bangle earrings, five piece brown composition baby body. Excellent condition.
Comments: Original ornamental necklace and skirt.
Courtesy of: Theriaults
Price Range: $375.00-600.00

Name: "No Name" Carribean Girl
Maker's Name: Heubach Koppelsdorf
Marks: Heubach Koppelsdorf 399 7/0 DRGM Germany
Origin: Germany
Size: 12"
Date: circa 1925
Description: Solid domed brown bisque socket head, painted black baby hair, tiny brown glass sleep eyes, painted black lashes, black tinted brows, broad modelled nose with sculpted nostrils, closed mouth with fully shaped lips, pierced ear, five piece brown papier-mache body. Excellent condition with original clothing (Carribean costume).
Comments: Heubach Koppelsdorf made the doll described, directed at the tourists in the Carribean Islands, originally costumed as a native child. Fine quality bisque.
Courtesy of: Theriaults
Price Range: $375.00-500.00

*Description of other dolls (far right), not available. (Both are made of composition.)

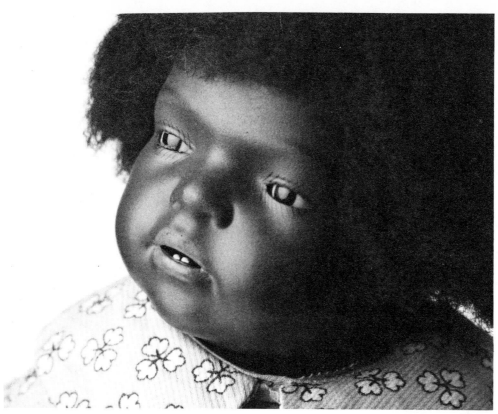

Name: "No Name" Female
Maker's Name: Heubach Koppelsdorf
Marks: Heubach Koppelsdorf 406.50 Germany
Origin: Germany
Size: 13"
Date: circa 1900-1920
Description: Brown bisque socket head with tiny black glass inset eyes, black painted curly lashes, short feathered brows, accent dots at eye corners and nostrils, open mouth, richly shaped lips, two lower teeth, black fleeced hair, composition five-piece toddler body with straight legs, well dressed. Excellent condition.
Comments: Soft Negroid features enhanced by the fine rich brown complexion with patina. All original. Rare.
Courtesy of: Theriaults
Price Range: $700.00-900.00

Name: "No Name" Female Girl
Maker's Name: Armand Marseille
Marks: Armand Marseille 390n Germany A4M. Armand Marseille, circa 1920
Origin: Germany
Size: 19"
Date: circa 1920
Description: Brown bisque socket head, brown glass sleep eyes, painted dark lashes, black feathered brows, accent dots at nostrils, open mouth, four teeth, black mohair wig, brown composition and wooden ball-jointed body, well dressed. Excellent condition.
Comments: *Fine oil lustre to brown bisque, which is not the common technique used to finish this model.
Courtesy of: Theriaults
Price Range: $1,350.00-1,750.00

Name: French Bebe′
Maker's Name: Societe Francais de Bebes et Jouets
Marks: Unis France 71 149 6/0
Origin: France
Size: 14"
Date: circa 1920
Description: Brown painted bisque socket head, green glass paperweight inset eyes, dark painted lashes, black feathered brows, accented nostrils, open mouth, shaded lips, black mohair with in little pigtails, five-piece brown papier mache body. Excellent condition.
Comments: Well made doll for a "late" (after 1910) "Bebe" doll. When the French doll companies formed SFBJ the quality began to waiver during the last decades of its existance (1920-30s).
Courtesy of: Theriaults
Price Range: $400.00-600.00

Name: "No Name" Female Girl (at top center)
Maker's Name: Kestner
Marks: Made in Germany B (in script)
Origin: Germany
Size: 12"
Date: circa 1900
Description: Brown bisque socket head, large brown glass sleep eyes, dark painted lashes, incised eyeliner, thick black brushstroked and feathered brows, accent dots at eye corners and nostrils, open mouth, shaded lips, four teeth, black fleeced hair over plaster pate, brown composition and wooden ball jointed body. Excellent condition.
Comments: A rare early Kestner doll in petite cabinet size, has rich dark brown complexion with dewy patina. Original clothing and scalloped hat.
Courtesy of: Theriaults
Price Range: $600.00-750.00

Name: Dream Baby (at top left)
Maker's Name: Armand Marseille
Marks: AM Germany 341 2/0
Origin: Germany
Size: 10"
Date: circa 1923
Description: Solid domed brown bisque head, painted black baby hair and one-stroke brows, tiny brown glass inset eyes, painted lashes, accent dots at eyes corners and nostrils, closed mouth, richly painted lips, pierced ears, brown composition bent limb baby body. Excellent condition.
Comments: This model has an unusual brown cafe-au-lait complexion. The doll is all original including the lithographed paper box with the labeling on the base "Neger".
Courtesy of: Theriaults
Price Range: $450.00-600.00

Name: "No Name" Female Toddler (at bottom left)
Maker's Name: Heubach Koppelsdorf
Marks: Heubach Koppelsdorf 399.17/0 Germany
Origin: Germany
Size: 7"
Date: circa 1920
Description: Solid domed dark brown bisque socket head, painted black baby hair and brows, black glass inset eyes, large accent dots at eye corners, broad shaped nostrils, closed mouth with full richly shaped lips, pierced ears with original bangle earrings, brown composition five-piece body. All original clothing and head wrap. Excellent condition.
Comments: Unusual small size.
Courtesy of: Theriaults
Price Range: $300.00-450.00

Name: Dream Baby (at bottom right)
Maker's Name: Armand Marseille
Marks: AM Germany 341
Origin: Germany
Size: 9"
Date: circa 1923
Description: Solid domed brown bisque head with flanged neck, lightly tinted dark baby hair and brows, brown glass sleep eyes, curly painted lashes, accent dots at eye corners and nostrils. Closed mouth with downcast pouty lips, muslin baby body with brown composition hands. Excellent condition.
Comments: Available and sought after.
Courtesy of: Theriaults
Price Range: $450.00-575.00

Name: French Bebe
Maker's Name: Paris Bebe
Marks: Paris Bebe Tete Dep. 3 (on the head) / Paris Bebe (plus Eiffel Tower mark on the body)
Origin: France
Size: 12½″
Date: circa 1890
Description: Brown bisque socket head, large brown glass paperweight inset eyes, dark painted lashes, incised eyeliner, delicately brushstroked brows, accented nostrils, closed mouth with softly shaded lips, pierced ears, brunette mohair wig, brown composition and wooden ball jointed body, well dressed in bronze silk French frock and bonnet. All original. Excellent condition.
Comments: Especially fine amber brown complexion in a petite cabinet size (12½″). Scarce.
Courtesy of: Theriaults
Price Range: $2,700.00-3,500.00

Name: "No Name" Female
Maker's Name: Madsen
Marks: MADSEN
Origin: Attributed to Germany
Size: 5¼"
Date: circa 1900-1920s
Description: Brown bisque fully jointed toddler doll with glass inset eyes, painted red lips, three pink pigtails. Excellent condition.
Comments: All original. Dolls of this type are plentiful but well made and marked examples from Germany are not as readily available.
Courtesy of: Angie's Doll Boutique
Price Range: $75.00-90.00

Name: "No Name" Female Toddler
Maker's Name: Japan (no company name)
Marks: MADE IN JAPAN
Origin: Japan
Size: 3½"
Date: circa 1920s
Description: Dark brown bisque jointed doll, molded and tinted hair with 2 pigtails of human hair, painted features and original knitted outfit. Excellent condition.
Comments: Common and plentiful.
Courtesy of: Davern Collection
Price Range: $45.00-75.00

Name: "No Name" Female Girl
Maker's Name: Unnamed
Marks: R. Dep. 9/0
Origin: Germany
Size: 10"
Date: circa 1900-1920s
Description: Bisque brown complexioned doll on a brown papier mache body, painted red lips, glass brown inset eyes, brushstroked eyebrows, braided fleeced hair, redressed. Very good condition. 5-piece jointed body.
Comments: Available
Courtesy of: Angie's Doll Boutique
Price Range: $110.00-175.00

Name: "No Name" Baby (at top center)
Maker's Name: Heubach Kopplesdorf
Marks: Heubach Kopplesdorf 399.3 Germany DRGM
Origin: Germany
Size: 19"
Date: circa 1925
Description: Brown bisque, solid domed socket head with soft matte complexion, black tinted baby hair and furrowed brows, black painted lashes, accent dots at eye corners and nostrils, closed mouth with somber pouty expression, softly shaded lips, pierced ears, brown composition, bent limb baby body. Excellent condition.
Comments: *Compare the finish/complexion of the doll described with that of (bottom right #399. 2/0).
Courtesy of: Theriaults
Price Range: $600.00-800.00

Name: Dream Baby (at bottom left)
Maker's Name: Armand Marseille
Marks: AM Germany 341/8/K
Origin: Germany
Size: 19"
Date: circa 1925
Description: Solid domed brown bisque head with tiny brown glass sleep eyes, dark painted lashes, black tinted hair and brows, accent dots at eye corners and nostrils, closed mouth, composition bent limb baby body, well dressed. Excellent condition.
Comments: A large model of the "Dream Baby". This example has a well blended tawny brown complexion and a socket head.
Courtesy of: Theriaults
Price Range: $800.00-1,000.00

Name: Dream Baby (at bottom center)
Maker's Name: Armand Marseille
Marks: AM, Germany 351 4/0
Origin: Germany
Size: 7½"
Date: circa 1925
Description: Solid domed brown bisque socket head, tiny brown glass sleep eyes, black tinted baby hair and brows, accent dots at eye corners and nostrils, closed mouth, 5-piece brown composition baby body with tiny folded fists. Excellent condition.
Comments: Petite model of the Dream Baby has a soft brown matte complexion, all original and well detailed chubby baby body, delicate shading of the hair.
Courtesy of: Theriaults
Price Range: $300.00-450.00

Name: "No Name" Baby (at bottom right)
Maker's Name: Heubach Kopplesdorf
Marks: Heubach Kopplesdorf 399.2/0 DRGM Germany
Origin: Germany
Size: 15"
Date: circa 1925
Description: Solid domed brown bisque socket head with shiny luster complexion, very narrow brown glass sleep eyes, painted curly lashes, black painted baby hair, furrowed brows with hint of color, accent dots at eye corners and nostrils of broadly sculpted nose, closed mouth with richly shaded lips, pierced ears, brown composition bent limb baby body, well dressed. Excellent condition.
Comments: Dramatic luster complexion.
Courtesy of: Theriaults
Price Range: $600.00-750.00

Name: "No Name" Female Toddler
Maker's Name: Japan (no company name)
Marks: JAPAN (on back and stamped on the diaper)
Origin: Japan
Size: 3¾"
Date: circa 1920s
Description: Dark brown bisque jointed toddler with painted features and 3 human hair tufts, all original clothing. Excellent condition.
Comments: Common and plentiful.
Courtesy of: Davern Collection
Price Range: $50.00-75.00

Name: "No Name" Female Toddler
Maker's Name: Japan (no company name)
Marks: MADE IN JAPAN
Origin: Japan
Size: 4"
Date: circa 1920s
Description: All bisque brown toddler adorned in a felt diaper with painted features and human hair tufts with molded baby hair. Fully jointed. Excellent condition.
Comments: Common and plentiful.
Courtesy of: Davern Collection
Price Range: $45.00-65.00

Name: "No Name" Female Toddler
Maker's Name: Japan (no company name)
Marks: JAPAN
Origin: Japan
Size: 4"
Date: circa 1920s
Description: All bisque dark brown toddler with painted features and molded tinted hair with 3 hair tufts. Fully jointed. All original. Excellent condition.
Comments: Common and plentiful.
Courtesy of: Davern Collection
Price Range: $45.00-75.00

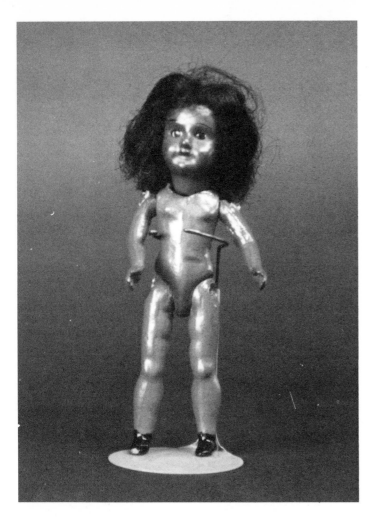

Name: "No Name" Female Girl
Maker's Name: SFBJ
Marks: None
Origin: France
Size: 8½"
Date: circa 1920s-1930s
Description: Bisque socket head doll with inset brown glass eyes, brushstroked brows, painted red lips and black painted boots. Human hair wig (brown). Rough 5-piece papier mache body. Good condition. (Undressed).
Comments: "Late" example of an SFBJ doll. Common but not plentiful.
Price Range: $350.00-450.00 *(All original and dressed)

Name: "No Name" Female Toddler
Maker's Name: Armand Marseille
Marks: A.M. Germany 990 A 9/0 M
Origin: Germany
Size: 7"
Date: circa 1920s
Description: Bisque socket head on a rough papier mache body (5-piece), brown sleep eyes, open mouth with 2 top teeth. Fully jointed with cloth attachments at the joints (chubby body). Good condition.
Comments: The doll described above came with a human hair wig and cotton clothing of various styles.
Price Range: $400.00-500.00 *(All original and dressed)

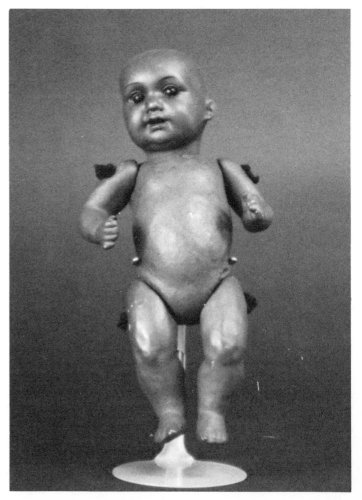

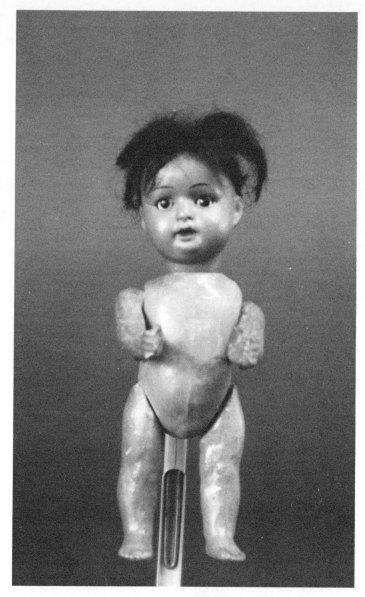

Name: Hanna
Maker's Name: Schoenau Hoffmeister
Marks: Germany S (star shape with P.B.) H Hanna 12/0
Origin: Germany
Size: 7"
Date: circa 1920s-1930s
Description: Light brown bisque socket head on a rough 5-piece papier mache body. Glass inset eyes, 1-stroke brows with open painted mouth. Human hair wig. Good condition. (Undressed).
Comments: Common and available.
Price Range: $300.00-450.00 *(All original and dressed)

Name: "No Name" Female Girl
Maker's Name: Heinrich Handwerck / Simon & Halbig
Marks: Simon/Halbig
Origin: Germany
Size: 18"
Date: circa 1900-1920
Description: Bisque socket head on a composition body, ball jointed, dimple on chin, black multi-stroked brows, glass brown sleep eyes, 4 upper teeth, human hair wig. Very good condition.
Comments: Available but not plentiful.
Price Range: $500.00-650.00

Name: "No Name" Female Young Lady
Maker's Name: Unmarked
Marks: 50 R. Dep 3/0 A X
Origin: France
Size: 13½"
Date: circa 1900-1920s
Description: Bisque socket head on a well designed papier mache body, jointed at the shoulders, hips, knees and elbows, brownish-orange glass eyes, 1-stroke brows, mohair wig and painted red lips. Excellent condition. (Re-dressed).
Comments: Available but not plentiful.
Price Range: $500.00-650.00

Name: "No Name" African Baby
Maker's Name: Heubach Koppelsdorf
Marks: 399 - ¹³/0 DRGM Germany
Origin: Germany
Size: 9½"
Date: circa 1900-1920s
Description: Solid dome brown bisque socket doll head on a chubby baby's body made of composition. Inset blue glass eyes, tinted black baby hair, closed mouth. Negroid features. Dressed in original lower torso wrap. Very good condition.
Comments: Common and available.
Price Range: $550.00-600.00

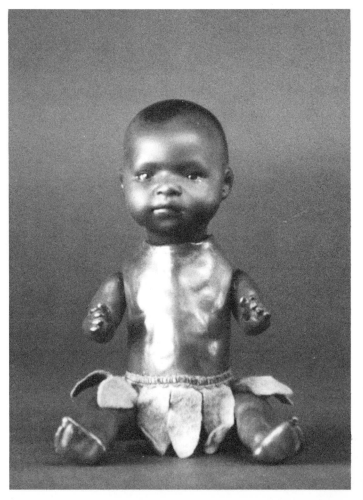

Name: Frozen Charlotte (or) Pillar Doll
Maker's Name: Unmarked
Marks: None
Origin: Germany
Size: 4″
Date: circa 1900-1910
Description: All bisque doll with molded painted features made in the image of a young female. Slightly exaggerated Negroid features. No moveable joints. Hairstyle is curled with a part in the middle. Very good condition. *Bisque with a rubbed oil finish.
Comments: Frozen Charlotte or Pillar Dolls were made circa mid-1800s-1920s. They were made in the image of and representative of a girl in a folk song that was frozen in her excitement to meet her beau on a cold winter's night. Black versions of this doll are available but not plentiful. Well made dressed versions in Black with detailed features are scarce.
Courtesy of: Yesteryear's Museum
Price Range: $125.00-160.00

Name: Frozen Charlie (or) Pillar Doll
Maker's Name: Unmarked
Marks: None
Origin: Germany
Size: 3¾″
Date: circa 1900-1910
Description: All bisque male doll with an oil rubbed finish, molded painted features, short molded curly hair and detailed body modeling. Bold naturalistic Negroid features. Excellent condition.
Comments: Good example of a nude Charlie. Available.
Courtesy of: Yesteryear's Museum
Price Range: $125.00-170.00

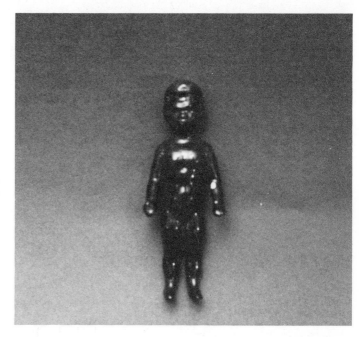

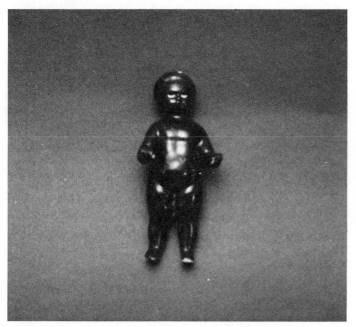

Name: Frozen Charlotte (or) Pillar Doll
Maker's Name: Unmarked
Marks: None
Origin: Germany
Size: 4″
Date: circa 1900-1910
Description: All bisque oil-rubbed female doll with the chubby Frozen Charlotte body. Slightly exaggerated Negroid features - molded and painted. Excellent condition.
Comments: Available but not plentiful.
Courtesy of: Yesteryear's Museum
Price Range: $125.00-160.00

Name: Hottentot (Kewpie)
Maker's Name: Unmarked
Marks: None
Origin: U.S.A.
Size: 6″
Date: circa 1920s
Description: Impish looking all black bisque chubby male doll with jointed arms and legs molded together. Side glancing painted eyes, red painted lips with white molded painted small wings attached to the upper back (shoulders). Molded-peaked tinted hair. Excellent condition.
Comments: Black version of the Kewpie doll created originally by Rose O'Neill, a writer, circa 1900s-1920s. Hottentots (Black Kewpies) are very scarce. Originals by Rose O'Neill with markings are rare. *Style varies, thus affects cost.
Courtesy of: Yesteryear's Museum
Price Range: $160.00-175.00 (unmarked) *Common style
$400.00-550.00 (Rose O'Neill)

Name: Pillar Doll
Maker's Name: Unmarked
Marks: None
Origin: Germany
Size: 2″
Date: circa 1880-1900
Description: All bisque oil-rubbed doll, molded and painted features and clothing. Negroid features. Excellent condition.
Comments: Available but not plentiful.
Courtesy of: Yesteryear's Museum
Price Range: $75.00-95.00

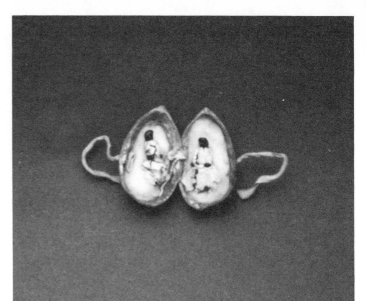

Name: Nutshell Dolls
Maker's Name: Germany (no company name)
Marks: Germany (on a small piece of printed paper)
Origin: Germany
Size: ¾″ each
Date: circa 1880-1900
Description: All bisque female dolls nestled in a nutshell on a bed of cotton. All original silk clothing. Faintly detailed features molded and painted. Excellent condition.
Comments: Rare size.
Courtesy of: Yesteryear's Museum
Price Range: $175.00-225.00

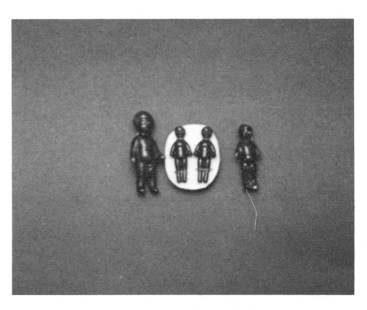

Name: Pillar Dolls
Maker's Name: Germany (no company name)
Marks: None
Origin: Germany
Size: 1⅜″ left, 1″ center (twins) & 1⅛″ far right
Date: circa 1880-1900
Description: All bisque oil-rubbed dolls of varying sizes. Faintly molded and painted Negroid features. All dolls in excellent condition.
Comments: Rare small sizes. The set of twins are perfectly matched on their original cardboard mount. Twins are scarce, made of any doll-material.
Courtesy of: Yesteryear's Museum
Price Range: $65.00-85.00 each (singles)
$75.00-90.00 (twins)

Name: "No Name" Female Girl
Maker's Name: Simon & Halbig
Marks: S & H Dep
Origin: Germany
Size: 19¾"
Date: circa 1890-1900
Description: Bisque head female doll with a composition fully jointed body (ball jointed). Open mouth with painted red lips, glass inset brown eyes, four teeth. Original clothing. Excellent condition. Human hair wig, pierced ears.
Comments: Non-ethnic features. Available but not plentiful.
Courtesy of: Yesteryear's Museum
Price Range: $600.00-750.00

Name: Dream Baby
Maker's Name: Armand Marseille
Marks: AM
Origin: Germany
Size: 10½"
Date: circa 1910-1920s
Description: Bisque brown head on a cloth body with composition arms. Brown glass inset eyes, painted red lips, domed head with tinted hairline. Original blanket and long white gown. Excellent condition.
Comments: Available but not plentiful.
Courtesy of: Yesteryear's Museum
Price Range: $650.00-775.00

Name: "No Name" Baby
Maker's Name: Heubach Koppelsdorf
Marks: Heubach / Koppelsdorf
Origin: Germany
Size: 6¾"
Date: circa 1920s
Description: Fully jointed brown bisque chubby body doll with a domed head displaying fine tinted baby hair, inset brown glass eyes, closed painted mouth (red). All original outfit, dressed in a native costume of the Islands. Excellent condition.
Comments: Dolls adorned in native costumes representing various countries were aimed at tourists. The doll described above is well made and made in an unusually small size.
Courtesy of: Yesteryear's Museum
Price Range: $300.00-425.00

Name: "No Name" Female Adult
Maker's Name: Marianne DeNunuz
Marks: Marianne DeNunuz 1966
Origin: U.S.A.
Size: 15½"
Date: 1966
Description: Brown bisque socket head and shoulder plate with a leather soft-brown body, jointed at the shoulders and knees. Original mohair wig and hand crafted beaded necklace, inset brown glass eyes. Excellent condition. (Undressed).
Comments: Fine example of Ms. DeNunuz's craftmanship.
Courtesy of: Yesteryear's Museum
Price Range: $225.00-300.00

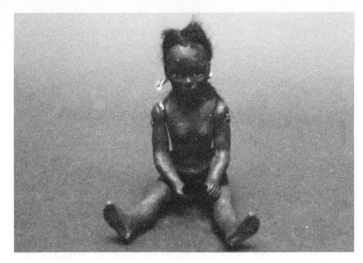

Name: "No Name" Female Young Adult
Maker's Name: A. Borigivee'
Marks: A Borigivee' (markings not completely legible)
Origin: Attributed to France
Size: 6"
Date: circa 1900-1920s
Description: Dark brown rough bisque female doll with painted molded features, fully jointed with animal hair attachements threaded and knotted through the limbs. Original fur skin skirt with a nude anatomically correct adult chest, human hair wig exhibiting very strong naturalistic Negroid features. Excellent condition.
Comments: Scarce
Courtesy of: Yesteryear's Museum
Price Range: $135.00-195.00

Name: "No Name" Female Girl
Maker's Name: Simon & Halbig
Marks: SHH Germany R
Origin: Germany
Size: 10"
Date: circa 1920s-1930s
Description: Bisque head doll with a composition body, fully jointed. Glass sleep eyes are nestled in the rich dark brown face, painted red lips, four teeth, red painted boots, fleeced wool wig. Good condition.
Comments: Common and plentiful.
Courtesy of: Angie's Doll Boutique
Price Range: $165.00-235.00

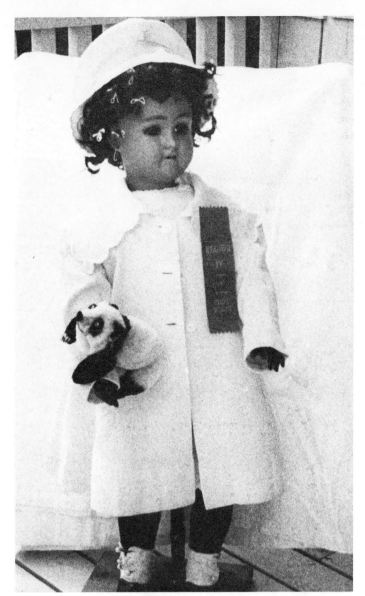

Name: "No Name" Female Girl
Maker's Name: Handwerk
Marks: S & H Handwerck MADE IN GERMANY 6½
Origin: Germany
Size: 32"
Date: circa 1890s-1900
Description: Medium brown bisque doll, fully jointed, molded facial features, brown glass eyes, black curly short human hair wig tied with tiny pink ribbons, pierced ears, painted orange lips with an open mouth and teeth. Long eye lashes and multi-stroked brows. Original clothing, white dress and coat/matching hat and high top leather shoes. Excellent condition.
Comments: Available. Well dressed. Non-ethnic features. *Head by Simon & Halbig. All original.
Courtesy of: Heidepriem Collector
Price Range: $1,750.00-2,300.00

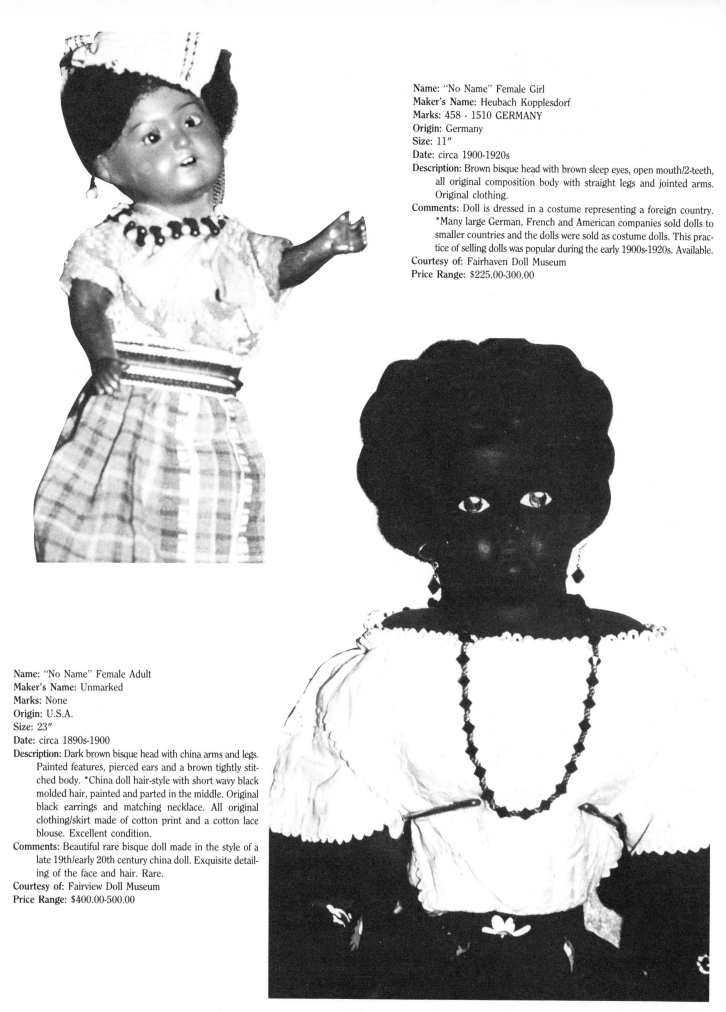

Name: "No Name" Female Girl
Maker's Name: Heubach Kopplesdorf
Marks: 458 - 1510 GERMANY
Origin: Germany
Size: 11"
Date: circa 1900-1920s
Description: Brown bisque head with brown sleep eyes, open mouth/2-teeth, all original composition body with straight legs and jointed arms. Original clothing.
Comments: Doll is dressed in a costume representing a foreign country. *Many large German, French and American companies sold dolls to smaller countries and the dolls were sold as costume dolls. This practice of selling dolls was popular during the early 1900s-1920s. Available.
Courtesy of: Fairhaven Doll Museum
Price Range: $225.00-300.00

Name: "No Name" Female Adult
Maker's Name: Unmarked
Marks: None
Origin: U.S.A.
Size: 23"
Date: circa 1890s-1900
Description: Dark brown bisque head with china arms and legs. Painted features, pierced ears and a brown tightly stitched body. *China doll hair-style with short wavy black molded hair, painted and parted in the middle. Original black earrings and matching necklace. All original clothing/skirt made of cotton print and a cotton lace blouse. Excellent condition.
Comments: Beautiful rare bisque doll made in the style of a late 19th/early 20th century china doll. Exquisite detailing of the face and hair. Rare.
Courtesy of: Fairview Doll Museum
Price Range: $400.00-500.00

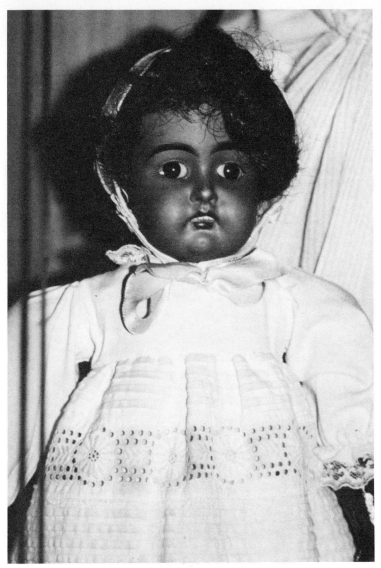

Name: "No Name" Female Girl
Maker's Name: Unmarked
Marks: GERMANY
Origin: Germany
Size: 16½"
Date: circa 1890s-1910
Description: Bisque head with brown stationary eyes. Black human hair wig, open
   mouth, 4 teeth and molded delicate features. Head is a soft medium brown,
   body is black composition ball and jointed. Excellent condition.
Comments: Well made doll. Available but not plentiful.
Courtesy of: Fairview Doll Museum
Price Range: $850.00-1,200.00

Name: "No Name" Female Adult
Maker's Name: Unmarked
Marks: None
Origin: France
Size: 27"
Date: circa 1900-1920s
Description: Brown bisque shoulder head with exquisite molded painted features with molded
   painted hair in tight curls, cotton stuffed cloth body. Original clothing in silks and
   satins. Excellent condition.
Comments: Available but not plentiful.
Courtesy of: Fairview Doll Museum
Price Range: $200.00-350.00

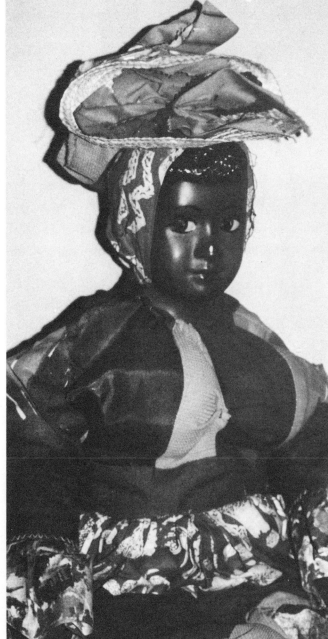

Name: No-Name
Maker's Name: Unmarked
Marks: None
Origin: Germany
Size: 5¾″
Date: circa 1890-1910
Description: Bisque-head papier mache doll with glass eyes, painted blue boots, red painted lips and mohair wig. Naturalistic features, entire body and face painted black. Excellent condition.
Comments: Common.
Courtesy of: Ron Carr Collection
Price Range: $200.00-300.00

Name: No-Name
Maker's Name: Unmarked
Marks: None
Origin: Germany
Size: 7¾″
Date: circa 1920-1940s
Description: All-bisque black painted doll with painted features, applied earrings. Jointed at the shoulders and hips. Original clothing. Excellent condition.
Comments: Plentiful.
Courtesy of: Ron Carr Collection
Price Range: $65.00-125.00

Name: No-Name
Maker's Name: Simon Halbig
Marks: Simon Halbig (SH in script)
Origin: Germany
Size: 17"
Date: circa 1900-1920s
Description: Bisque head with composition body painted a medium brown. Human hair wig, open mouth with four upper teeth, dark brown sleep eyes with multi-stroke brows, deep dimple in the chin, 15 pc. ball and jointed body. Redressed. Excellent condition.
Comments: Common but not plentiful in the "Black" versions.
Price Range: $650.00-800.00

Name: No-Name
Maker's Name: A Lanternier & Cie. of Limoges, France
Marks: Lanternier
Origin: France
Size: 21½"
Date: circa 1900-1920s
Description: Excellent condition.
Comments: Bisque head doll with a rough textured papier mache body painted medium brown. Brown stationery glass eyes with multi-stroke brows, faint dimple in the chin, open mouth with five teeth. Wooden painted arms and legs, ball jointed. Redressed. Excellent condition.
Courtesy of: Common but not plentiful.
Price Range: $1,100.00-$1,400.00

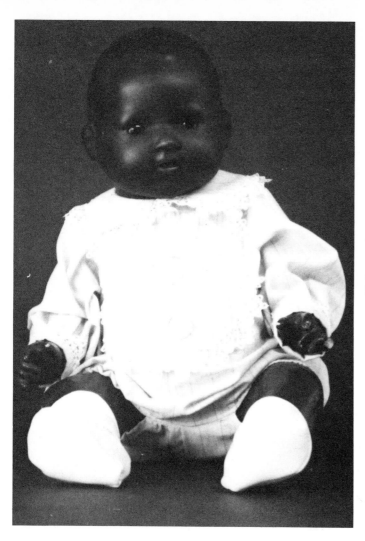

Name: Kiddiejoy
Maker's Name: Armand Marseille
Marks: A.M. Germany 351/8K
Origin: Germany
Size: 20″
Date: circa 1900-1920s
Description: Bisque dome-head baby with a brown painted composition body. Sleep brown eyes, open mouth with two lower teeth, fully jointed with bent legs, five-piece body. Redressed. Excellent condition.
Comments: Common but not plentiful in "Black" versions.
Price Range: $1,100.00-1,350.00

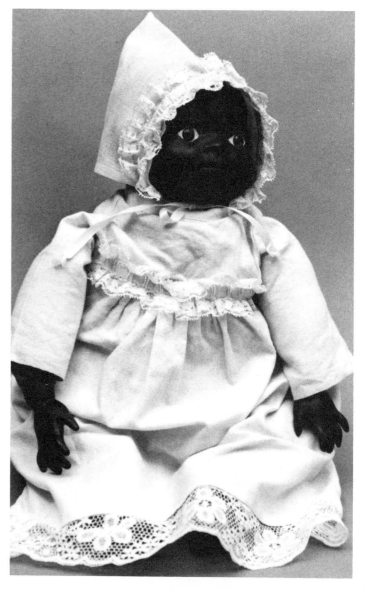

Name: Bye-Lo Baby **Reproduction
Maker's Name: **Reproduced mold name only (Putnam)
Marks: Grace Storey Putnam, Bye-Lo
Origin: U.S.A.
Size: 19″
Date: circa 1960
Description: Reproduction black painted bisque doll with molded features, glassine eyes, original clothes. Excellent condition.
Comments: Plentiful.
Courtesy of: Ron Carr Collection
Price Range: $125.00-160.00

Name: Hottentot (Kewpie)
Maker's Name: Germany
Marks: GERMANY
Origin: Germany
Size: 5″
Date: circa 1900-1920s
Description: All-bisque black painted Kewpie doll referred to as a "Hottentot". Jointed arms. Blue molded painted wings on the upper back of the doll.
Comments: Common but not plentiful.
Courtesy of: V. Mackemull Collection
Price Range: $400.00-500.00

Name: No-Name
Maker's Name: Unmarked
Marks: None
Origin: Germany
Size: 6½″
Date: circa 1900-1920s
Description: All-bisque black painted doll, fully jointed, glass eyes, wool wig. Original clothing. Excellent condition.
Comments: Common.
Courtesy of: V. Mackemull Collection
Price Range: $140.00-175.00

Name: No-Name
Maker's Name: Unmarked
Marks: None
Origin: Germany
Size: 4½″
Date: circa 1920s-1930s
Description: All-bisque jointed shoulders, hips, head, brown painted dolls with molded, painted hair and features. Ethnic features. Excellent condition.
Comments: Common.
Courtesy of: M. Davern Collection
Price Range: $65.00-80.00

Name: No-Name
Maker's Name: Unmarked
Marks: None
Origin: Germany
Size: 5½″ each
Date: circa 1890s-1920s
Description: All-bisque dolls jointed at the shoulders. Molded, painted features with molded necklaces and skirts. One doll is light brown and the other is painted black. Excellent condition.
Comments: Common.
Courtesy of: V. Mackemull Collection
Price Range: $200.00-350.00 (pair)

Name: No-Name
Maker's Name: Unmarked
Marks: None
Origin: Japan
Size: 5″
Date: circa 1920s-1930s
Description: Brown painted bisque girl and boy dolls with jointed legs and arms and turning heads. Boy's hair molded and painted. Girl's hair is mohair wig. Both dolls have molded painted features. Excellent condition.
Comments: Common.
Courtesy of: M. Davern Collection
Price Range: $85.00-100.00 (pair)

Name: No-Name
Maker's Name: Unmarked
Marks: None
Origin: Germany
Size: 4¼″
Date: circa 1900-1915
Description: All-bisque fully jointed doll with molded painted features, painted boots, original mohair wig and clothing. Doll is a medium brown color. Excellent condition.
Comments: Scarce.
Price Range: $300.00-400.00

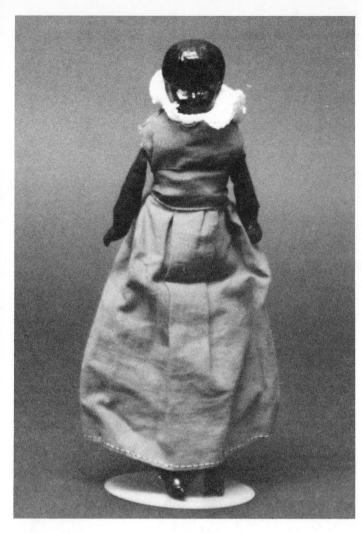

Name: No-Name
Maker's Name: Unmarked
Marks: None
Origin: U.S.A.
Size: 9″
Date: circa 1880-1920s
Description: A painted black china doll fired (glaze) with molded painted features. Black pupils and red lips. China head, hands and feet with a well made mellow brown body. Redressed. Good condition.
Comments: Common but not plentiful.
Courtesy of: M. Davern Collection
Price Range: $125.00-175.00

Name: No-Name
Maker's Name: Japan
Marks: JAPAN
Origin: Japan
Size: 2½″ each
Date: circa 1920s-1930s
Description: All-bisque dolls painted brown with molded painted clothing and shoes. Hair is molded with human hair pigtails. Both dolls have molded painted features. Excellent condition.
Comments: Common.
Courtesy of: M. Davern Collection
Price Range: $50.00-75.00 each

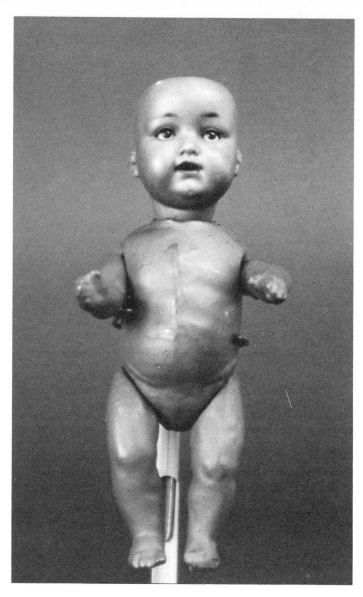

Name: No-Name
Maker's Name: Armand Marseille
Marks: Armand Marseille A.M.
Origin: Germany
Size: 9″
Date: circa 1900-1920s
Description: Bisque-head toddler with a composition body. Jointed body with a socket head. Light brown head with a medium brown body. Open mouth with two upper teeth. Open "pate" head (hole is visible). Good condition.
Comments: Common.
Price Range: $165.00-225.00 (excellent condition)

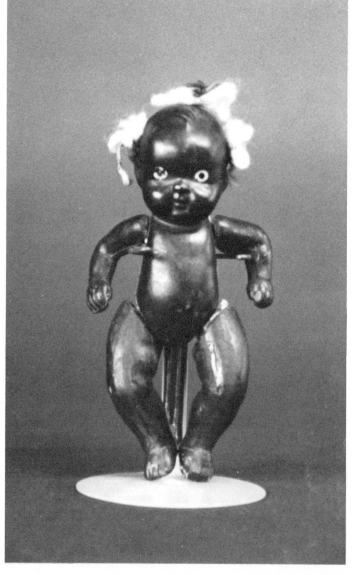

Name: No-Name
Maker's Name: Japan
Marks: JAPAN
Origin: Japan
Size: 6″
Date: circa 1900-1930s
Description: All-bisque black painted doll with jointed arms and legs (strung). Molded painted features with tufts of hair pulled through three holes in the doll's head (pigtails). Dark brown painted body. Good condition.
Comments: Plentiful.
Price Range: $45.00-75.00

Wood and Odd Materials

Dolls

Name: "No Name" Female Adult
Maker's Name: Unmarked
Marks: None
Origin: U.S.A.
Size: 3½"
Date: circa 1900-1920s
Description: Rubber nipple doll with a painted head and painted features. Clothing is all original with head kerchief. Doll holds a broom in one hand. Excellent condition.
Comments: Available but not plentiful.
Courtesy of: Yarmouth County Museum
Price Range: $65.00-85.00

Name: Pullman Conductor
Maker's Name: Unmarked
Marks: None
Origin: U.S.A.
Size: 20"
Date: circa 1870s-1890s
Description: An all hand carved wooden doll with caricature features depicting an adult Black man, one-piece wooden head and torso with elongated slender modelling, jointed at the shoulders, hips and knees, carved fingers and toes. Full carved ears, eyes, mouth and flared nostrils. The mouth is open with carved painted white teeth. Original black fleece wig and clothing (black wool suit and conductor cap with a red bow tie). Excellent condition.
Comments: The doll described was crafted by an imaginative artist of great skill. Rare.
Courtesy of: Theriaults
Price Range: $1,400.00-1,800.00

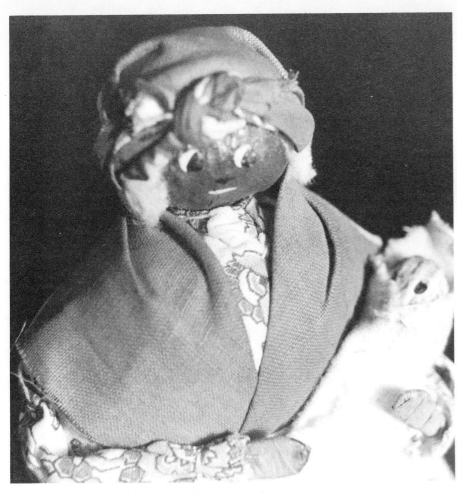

Name: "No Name" Female Adult
Maker's Name: Unmarked
Marks: None
Origin: U.S.A.
Size: 7⅝"
Date: circa 1900-1920s
Description: Black adult female, chestnut head with painted face, wire limbs wrapped with paper, stuffed upper torso, there are no legs but instead a stick which attaches to torso and square wood base or stand. Baby is held in the larger doll's arms. *Baby is made of a peanut and wrapped in a cloth blanket. Baby's features are painted. Both dolls are all original. Very good condition. (Bathroom fixtures not included with dolls).
Comments: Available
Courtesy of: Lighter Museum
Price Range: $80.00-100.00

Name: Vargas (type)
Maker's Name: Attributed to Vargas
Marks: None
Origin: U.S.A. (New Orleans)
Size: 6½"
Date: circa 1940s-1960s
Description: Brown wax figure of a man with sculptured features and original clothing. The strong Negroid features are enhanced by the characater's expression. Bundles of straw/cane are on the back of the character and another bundle is at the figure's feet. Curly human hair wig. Excellent condition.
Comments: Well made doll.
Courtesy of: Dolly Wares Doll Museum
Price Range: $85.00-100.00

Name: "No Name" Female Adult
Maker's Name: Unmarked
Marks: None
Origin: U.S.A.
Size: 4⅜"
Date: circa 1910-1930
Description: Nut head with painted features on a brown cloth body dressed in a matronly outfit (shawl, apron, dress and head kerchief). Excellent condition.
Comments: Available but not plentiful from the early 20th and late 19th centuries.
Courtesy of: Angie's Doll Boutique
Price Range: $45.00-60.00

Name: "No Name" Female Girl
Maker's Name: Unmarked
Marks: None
Origin: U.S.A.
Size: 6¼"
Date: circa 1930s-1950s
Description: Nut head female with painted features, black yarn hair, wire body and original clothing. Excellent condition.
Comments: Available
Courtesy of: Angie's Doll Boutique
Price Range: $35.00-55.00

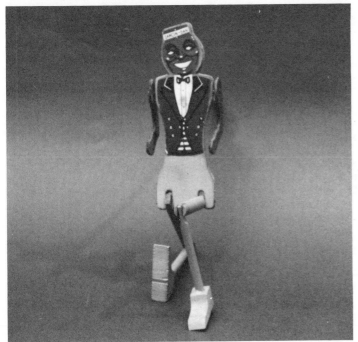

Name: Dancin-Dan
Maker's Name: Unmarked
Marks: (name on head) DANCIN-DAN
Origin: U.S.A.
Size: 11¾"
Date: circa 1920s
Description: All wooden, jointed male doll with additional knee joints, lithographed features and clothing. Character appears in a cap with "name" on the brim, suited in a vest-shirt and bow tie. The flat surfaced body has rounded legs and flat hinged arms. The doll has a smiling face with teeth showing and side glancing eyes. Excellent condition.
Comments: Dancing doll from the 1920s are available and fairly accessible.
Courtesy of: Angie's Doll Boutique
Price Range: $95.00-135.00

Name: "No Name Marionette" Male Boy
Maker's Name: Unmarked
Marks: None
Origin: U.S.A.
Size: 8½"
Date: circa 1915-1930s
Description: Wooden, carved, dark brown male with strong Negroid features slightly exaggerated and painted, hair is realistically arranged and painted (carved). The doll has an open mouth with carved painted teeth, defined body and carefully carved toes and feet. Strings are attached at the head, knees and arms. Excellent condition.
Comments: Scarce
Courtesy of: Angie's Doll Boutique
Price Range: $145.00-190.00

Name: "No Name" Female Adult
Maker's Name: Unmarked
Marks: None
Origin: U.S.A.
Size: 8½"
Date: circa 1890s-1920
Description: Buck-eye head with painted features attached to a body made of tobacco leaves, wearing a finely woven straw shawl and matching wide brim hat. The body of this doll is carefully layered tobacco leaves built up to form the surface clothing.
Comments: Scarce
Courtesy of: Angie's Doll Boutique
Price Range: $145.00-185.00

Name: "No Name" Female
Maker's Name: Unmarked
Marks: None
Origin: U.S.A.
Size: 6¼"
Date: circa 1930s-1950s
Description: Pecan head with painted features. Wire frame body and arms. Original clothing and head kerchief. Very good condition.
Comments: Available
Courtesy of: Angie's Doll Boutique
Price Range: $75.00-95.00

Name: Nipple Doll
Maker's Name: Unmarked
Marks: None
Origin: U.S.A.
Size: 3½"
Date: circa 1900-1910
Description: Rubber nipple painted to resemble a female adult with a kerchief on her head and a hand stitched print dress with a cotton lace apron. Stuffed sleeves are representing the arms. The doll is caricature in style. Wood fleece tuft used as hair. Excellent condition.
Comments: Scarce. Well dressed.
Courtesy of: Angie's Doll Boutique
Price Range: $75.00-95.00

Name: "No Name" Female Adult
Maker's Name: Unmarked
Marks: None
Origin: U.S.A.
Size: 4½"
Date: circa 1910-1940s
Description: Pin cushion doll with a wooden head and cloth stuffed body. Painted features, wool black hair. Caricature in style. Excellent condition.
Comments: Available
Courtesy of: Angie's Doll Boutique
Price Range: $35.00-50.00

Name: Ramp Walker
Maker's Name: Unmarked
Marks: None
Origin: U.S.A.
Size: 4⅝"
Date: circa 1910-1930s
Description: Wooden head with painted features in caricature style, wooden hands and legs attached to a stiff paper body. Original clothing and head kerchief. Doll walks when touched gently on the head in short intervals. Excellent condition.
Comments: Available. Doll is propelled by gravity.
Courtesy of: Angie's Doll Boutqique
Price Range: $55.00-85.00

Name: "No Name" Male Adult
Maker's Name: Unmarked
Marks: None
Origin: U.S.A.
Size: 5″
Date: circa 1910-1930s
Description: All wooden jointed hand-carved male doll tinted black with strong Negroid features. Painted carved facial features. Excellent condition.
Comments: Scarce. Well made.
Courtesy of: Angie's Doll Boutique
Price Range: $95.00-155.00

Name: "No Name" Adult Female and Baby
Maker's Name: Unmarked
Marks: None
Origin: U.S.A.
Size: 3¼″
Date: circa 1910-1930s
Description: Buck-eye head with painted features, cloth body with original dress and head kerchief. The adult doll is holding a 1½″ celluloid White baby. Good condition.
Comments: Available
Courtesy of: Angie's Doll Boutique
Price Range: $65.00-100.00

Name: "No Name" Male Adult
Maker's Name: Unmarked
Marks: None
Origin: U.S.A.
Size: 10¾″
Date: circa 1910-1940s
Description: Buck-eye head with painted features, cloth over wire body, original clothing-suspender pants, shirt and hat, wooden cane, burlap bag with unwoven cotton spilling out, stockinett feet and gray wool wig. Doll portrays an elderly gentleman. Excellent condition.
Comments: Available but not plentiful as male dolls, well dressed.
Courtesy of: Davern Collection
Price Range: $65.00-100.00

Name: "No Name" Female Adult
Maker's Name: Unmarked
Marks: None
Origin: U.S.A.
Size: 6½"
Date: circa 1920s-1940s
Description: Buck-eye head with painted features corn shuck body with original cotton apron and bonnet. Excellent condition.
Comments: Available
Courtesy of: Davern Collection
Price Range: $55.00-75.00

Name: Ramp Walkers
Maker's Name: Unmarked
Marks: None
Origin: U.S.A.
Size: 4½"

Comments: Available. *Lithographed faces are older.
Courtesy of: Davern Collection
Price Range: $55.00-75.00 each

Date: circa 1930s-1940s (left to right), circa 1920s (far right)
Description: Wooden dolls propelled by touching, painted features on the first 3 dolls from the left. Lithographed face on the far right doll. Wooden hands and feet, original clothing and head kerchief. All in good to excellent condition.

Name: Mechanical French Male Adult
Maker's Name: Unmarked
Marks: None
Origin: France
Size: 26¾″
Date: circa 1860-1890s
Description: Wooden mechanical male doll with fully jointed body and original clothing and hat. Finely detailed features, partially open molded eyes, lips and articulated fingers and toes (bare feet). The doll has a mechanism inside of his cardboard chest that when activated causes him to raise and lower his pipe to his mouth and pats his tummy with the opposite hand. Animal fur wig, brown glass eyes and six carved painted teeth. Very good condition.
Comments: Excellent French mechanical doll. Rare.
Courtesy of: Yesteryear's Museum
Price Range: $6,500.00-7,500.00

Name: Ring Master
Maker's Name: Shoenhut
Marks: Unmarked
Origin: U.S.A.
Size: 8¾″
Date: circa 1900-1910
Description: Wooden spring-hinged male doll with wooden claw-type hands, molded feet/shoes, painted and molded features, felt coat with cloth cotton shirt, pants and paper top hat. Excellent condition.
Comments: The doll described is a part of a set of circus characters and animals.
Courtesy of: Yesteryear's Museum
Price Range: $250.00-325.00

Name: "No Name" Female Girl
Maker's Name: Unmarked
Marks: None
Origin: Origin unknown, possibly Australian
Size: 5″
Date: circa 1875-1890s
Description: All wooden doll, carved and painted brown. Doll has strong Negroid features masterfully rendered in a naturalistic style. Animal fur wig, strip of cloth on the torso, fully jointed. Excellent condition.
Comments: The doll described is an excellent example of a late 19th century wooden doll. Detailed features this finely executed are rarely found on a doll as small as this 5″ example. Rare.
Courtesy of: Yarmouth County Museum
Price Range: $350.00-450.00

Name: "No Name" Female Adult
Maker's Name: Unmarked
Marks: None
Origin: U.S.A.
Size: 19″
Date: circa 1880s-1900
Description: Cotton canvas doll with a black head and painted features. Tightly sewn cotton body, black painted hands with stitched fingers. Original top (blouse) made of printed cotton. (No other clothing). Very good condition.
Comments: Scarce
Courtesy of: Yarmouth County Museum
Price Range: $350.00-450.00

Name: Fiji Family
Maker's Name: Unmarked
Marks: None
Origin: Fiji Islands
Size: Male 3″, Female 2″, Child 1″
Date: circa 1890s-1900
Description: Handmade dolls of dyed spun wool. The faces and bodies are charcoal black with a lighter color for the head decorations. Silk thread is used for clothing and the male's legs (silk wrapped). Excellent condition.
Comments: Rare
Courtesy of: Yarmouth County Museum
Price Range: $275.00-400.00 (set of 3)

Name: Aunt Jemima Family (Wade-boy, Diana-girl)
Maker's Name: Unmarked
Marks: None
Origin: U.S.A.
Size: 10″ each
Date: circa 1920-1930s
Description: Paper dolls from the Aunt Jemima family. They are all original, placed in a modern frame for display. Excellent condition.
Comments: Available but not plentiful in unplayed with condition.
Courtesy of: The Paper Pile, San Anselmo, California
Price Range: $15.00-$30.00 each (doll only)

Name: Nipple doll
Maker's Name: Unmarked
Marks: None
Origin: U.S.A.
Size: 4″
Date: circa 1910-1920s
Description: Doll made from an old baby bottle nipple and dressed to resemble a matronly lady. The doll has painted features. She holds a small white celluloid baby doll. Both dolls are in good condition.
Comments: Common but not plentiful.
Courtesy of: The Paper Pile, San Anselmo, California
Price Range: $65.00-75.00

Name: No-Name
Maker's Name: Unmarked
Marks: None
Origin: Western (U.S.A. or England)
Size: 8¾″
Date: circa 1840s-1860s
Description: All hand-made wooden, jointed-motise and tendon articulated doll. Arms are hinged with wire. Mortise and tendon joints at the knees, curved elbows, pelt skull cap-wig with animal fur, moveable feet with metal pin attachments. Carved features, mother of pearl inset eyes, carved teeth. Original clothing. Excellent condition.
Comments: Scarce.
Courtesy of: Ron Carr Collection
Price Range: $650.00-850.00

Name: Sambo and Mammy
Maker's Name: Florida Souvenirs
Marks: Florida Souvenirs
Origin: U.S.A.
Size: 12″
Date: circa© 1941
Description: Gourd-head "Sambo" and "Mammy" dolls with soft bodies, wooden hands
    and feet and painted features, head painted black. All original. Excellent condition.
Comments: Common.
Courtesy of: Ron Carr Collection
Price Range: $350.00-450.00 (pair)

Name: No-Name
Maker's Name: Unmarked
Marks: None
Origin: U.S.A.
Size: 5″, 2½″
Date: circa 1935-1945
Description: Both dolls are made of cloth and pipe cleaner wire. They have cloth
    heads and wire bodies. The large doll is made of brown cloth; the small doll
    represents a white baby. The dolls have stitched features. Good condition.
Comments: Plentiful.
Courtesy of: M. Davern Collection
Price Range: $25.00-50.00

Cloth Dolls

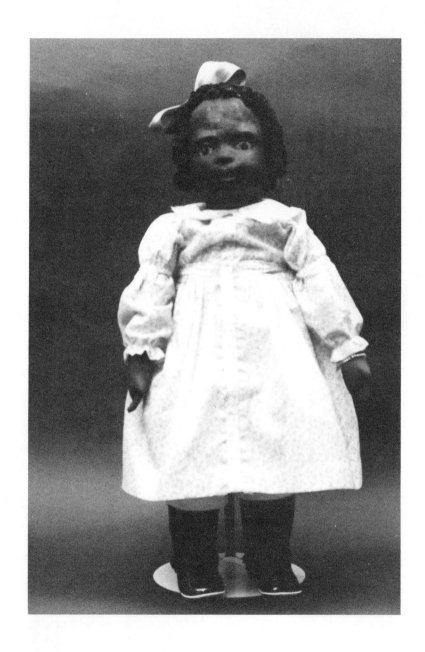

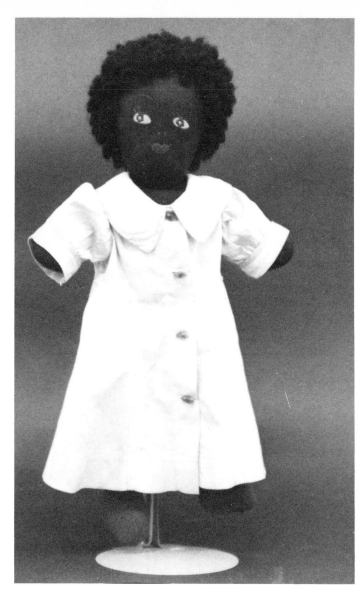

Name: "No Name" Female Girl
Maker's Name: Unmarked
Marks: None
Origin: U.S.A. (Philadelphia)
Size: 20″
Date: circa 1900-1930
Description: Satin black body-doll with tightly curled black yarn hair, stitched facial features. All original clothing and satin shoes (boots). Excellent condition.
Comments: Available, not plentiful.
Courtesy of: Charlene Upham
Price Range: $175.00-275.00

Name: "No Name" Female Adult
Maker's Name: Unmarked
Marks: None
Origin: U.S.A.
Size: 10″
Date: circa 1920s-1930s
Description: Medium brown female doll with a lithographed face, open mouth, silk thread black hair. Doll wears a grass skirt and arm and leg leis. Cloth flower on her head with a matching strapless top. All original. Excellent condition.
Comments: Available
Courtesy of: Silver Springs "Museum"
Price Range: $75.00-100.00

Name: "No Name" Female Girl
Maker's Name: Unmarked
Marks: None
Origin: U.S.A.
Size: 7⅜"
Date: circa 1900-1920s
Description: Brown yarn doll with twisted black
        yarn hair, black yarn eyes with white thread
        stars in them. Yarn mouth. Yarn dress with
        matching hat. All original. Excellent
        condition.
Comments: Available
Courtesy of: Lightner Museum
Price Range: $65.00-85.00

Name: "No Name" Female Adult
Maker's Name: Unmarked
Marks: None
Origin: U.S.A.
Size: 5½"
Date: circa 1930s-1940s
Description: Black cloth wrapped clothes pin adult doll with
        embroidered features, silver hoop earrings. Original
        clothing, carrying a straw purse. Excellent condition.
Comments: Available
Courtesy of: Lightner Museum
Price Range: $50.00-70.00

Name: "No Name" Female Girl   Comments: Available
Maker's Name: Roxie   Courtesy of: Lightner Museum
Marks: A Roxie doll (tag)   Price Range: $105.00-140.00
Origin: U.S.A.
Size: 12¼"
Date: circa 1920s-1940s
Description: Young female, dark brown cloth, stitched features, flat tightly
        sewn body. All original clothing with matching cloth shoes. Hair is
        in multiple braids with ribbons tied on the yarn wig. Very good
        condition.

Name: "No Name" Female Adult
Maker's Name: Attributed to Sisters of Mercy / Sanford, Maine
Marks: None
Origin: U.S.A.
Size: 19½"
Date: circa 1907-1908
Description: All cloth cotton stuffed, fabric made of a black sateen or polished cotton. Tightly stitched, wool hair (black), embroidered features. Redressed in the 1970s. Excellent condition.
Comments: Well made. Available.
Courtesy of: DAR Museum
Price Range: $175.00-225.00

Name: "No Name" Female Young Girl
Maker's Name: Unmarked
Marks: None
Origin: U.S.A.
Size: 11½"
Date: circa 1900-1920s
Description: Black young female, dark brown cloth with stitched features, silk thread hair (was braided at one time). Original dress, carrying a bouquet of flowers. Doll is handmade. Very good condition.
Comments: Available
Courtesy of: Lightner Museum
Price Range: $150.00-200.00

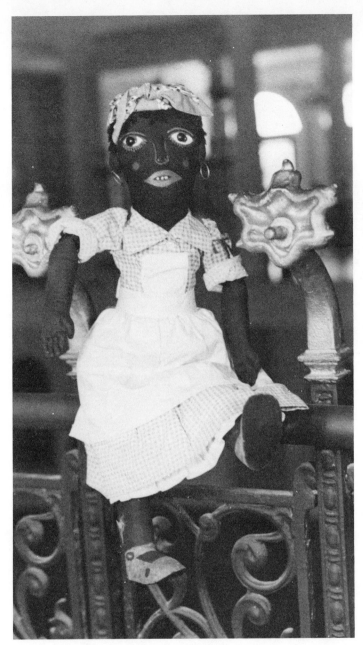

Name: "No Name" Female Adult
Maker's Name: B.A.L. CONKIAN DOLL BABIES
Marks: B.A.L. CONKLAN DOLL BODIES (on tag on back)
Origin: U.S.A.
Size: 21½″
Date: circa 1900-1910
Description: Black female, stuffed cloth body, limbs and head, bendable elbows, painted features, bead eyes, stitched nose, yarn hair, red bandana, gold hoop earrings, painted brown shoes and all original clothing. Excellent condition.
Comments: Well made. Available.
Courtesy of: Lightner Museum
Price Range: $160.00-225.00

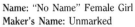
Name: "No Name" Female Girl
Maker's Name: Unmarked
Marks: None
Origin: U.S.A.
Size: 12½″
Date: circa 1930s-1950s
Description: All cloth doll with stitched features and black yarn hair. Original clothing. Excellent condition.
Comments: Common style. Plentiful.
Courtesy of: Angie's Doll Boutique
Price Range: $65.00-85.00

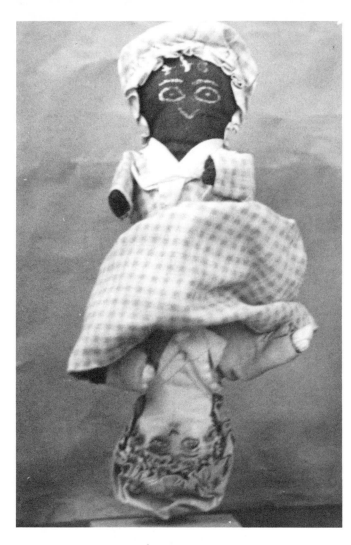

Name: Topsy Turvy
Maker's Name: Unmarked
Marks: None
Origin: U.S.A.
Size: 12″
Date: circa 1900-1920s
Description: All cloth double-end doll (one White and one Black). The Black doll is made of black cloth. Both doll ends have painted crude features, plain cotton dresses with matching night-bonnets. Very good condition.
Comments: Crude examples unrelated to age. Available.
Courtesy of: Dolly Wares Doll Museum
Price Range: $90.00-125.00

Name: Golly Wog
Maker's Name: Norah Wellings Productions
Marks: (original tag) NORAH WELLINGS PRODUCTIONS
Origin: England
Size: 13″
Date: circa 1920s-1940s
Description: Brown velvet head and hands. Painted molded features. Smiling expression with teeth. Feet are molded into the shape of shoes. All original clothing. Excellent condition.
Comments: Signed Norah Wellings' creations are available but not plentiful.
Courtesy of: Dolly Wares Doll Museum
Price Range: $135.00-175.00 (Allow $25.00 more for glass eyes)

Name: Brazilian Bahai Doll
Maker's Name: Unmarked
Marks: None
Origin: Brazil
Size: 15″
Date: circa 1800-1850s
Description: All cloth female adult made of black tightly sewn cloth with molded, stitched features, applied cloth nose, sculptured mouth with painted teeth. *Fingers on this doll are stitched and finely articulated with human fingernails. The feet are shaped and stitched. All original clothing (elaborately dressed), decorated with jewelry on her neck, ears and rings on her fingers. Original head dress. Excellent condition.
Comments: Rare. Extremely well made cloth dolls as described above are rare when found from any country.
Courtesy of: Dolly Wares Doll Museum
Price Range: $550.00-750.00

Name: Golliwog (left)
Maker's Name: The English Toy Company
Marks: Merrythought Ironbridge Shops (*original label)
Origin: England
Size: 14″
Description: All original, all cloth novelty doll with black velvet shaped head, celluloid bulging eyes, applique felt
   wide smile (red), black straight up-swept hair, yellow velvet stitched on shirt, black/white cotton stitched on
   trousers with red velvet jacket and black gloves. Excellent condition. Original label.
Comments: Child's storybook character created during the 1930s. Dolls were made in England and the U.S.A.
Courtesy of: Theriaults
Price Range: $165.00-225.00

Information for non-black dolls not available.

120

Name: Norah Wellings' Carribean Child
Maker's Name: Norah Wellings
Marks: Made in England by Norah Wellings
Origin: England
Size: 15″
Date: circa 1935
Description: Carribean child with a brown velvet swivel head, brown velvet body, black yarn hair, wearing a grass skirt and headdress, brown glass inset eyes, smiling-painted features and molded face.
Comments: The Norah Wellings' dolls were designed and made by her during the early to mid twentieth century.
Courtesy of: Theriaults
Price Range: $275.00-325.00

Information for non-black dolls not available.

Name: American Cloth Doll
Maker's Name: Art Fabric Mills
Marks: Art Fabric Mills Patented Feb. 13 1900
Origin: U.S.A.
Size: 18″
Date: circa 1900
Description: Muslin cut-out doll with lithographed hair, face and costume depicts a young Black baby with curly black hair, brown eyes, richly shaped pale lips, blue night smock with scalloped collar and open buttons, delineated fingers and toenails.
Comments: Scarce
Courtesy of: Theriaults
Price Range: $650.00-750.00

Information for non-black dolls not available.

Name: "No Name" Male and Female - Children
Maker's Name: Unmarked
Marks: None
Origin: U.S.A.
Size: 20½″ (both dolls)
Date: circa 1940-1960
Description: Both have brown yarn hair, stitched black eyebrows with silk thread, brown stitched eyes, red stitched mouth and black stitched dots for nostrils. Female dressed in a dress printed with white stars and blue pinafore/brown background on dress. Male has matching outfit with "star print" shirt and blue overalls. Both have dark brown lithographed shoes. Both all cloth dolls. Excellent condition.
Comments: Unusual matched pair.
Courtesy of: Angie's Doll Boutique
Price Range: $150.00-200.00 pair

Name: "No Name" Male and Female - Adults
Maker's Name: Unmarked
Marks: None
Origin: U.S.A.
Size: Male 18″, Female 16½″
Date: circa 1860-1880
Description: Both dolls are made of satin stockinette. Male doll has mohair wig, sewn purple thread eyelashes with white stitched eyes, cotton stuffed body, molded nose with red stitched mouth. Original clothing with wool pants, geometric design shirt and leather shoes and belt-tie style with straw-brim hat. Female has mohair wig, cotton stuffed body, stitched eyes and mouth of red thread with black dots for pupils, molded nose. All original printed dress with apron, headdress and scarf. *Both dolls have separate fingers with stitched fingernails. Female has earrings and cloth shoes (not original). Excellent condition.
Comments: Excellent examples of handmade 19th century dolls.
Courtesy of: Angie's Doll Boutique
Price Range: $350.00-400.00 pair

Name: "No Name" Female - Girl
Maker's Name: Unmarked
Marks: None
Origin: U.S.A.
Size: 6¾"
Date: circa 1940s
Description: Cloth doll with original cotton dress. Yarn bows on head, arms and ankles. Black yarn hair, white thread eyes, nose and mouth of red. Excellent condition.
Comments: Common doll-type.
Courtesy of: Angie's Doll Boutique
Price Range: $35.00-55.00

Name: "No Name" Female - Girl
Maker's Name: Unmarked
Marks: None
Origin: U.S.A.
Size: 7⅜"
Date: circa 1940-1950
Description: All cloth brown girl doll dressed in a print dress with a white apron and matching head scarf and neck scarf. Black yarn hair, painted white eyes, applied red felt lips and red dots for nostrils. Excellent condition.
Comments: Common doll-type.
Courtesy of: Angie's Doll Boutique
Price Range: $35.00-50.00

Name: "No Name" Female - Young Lady
Maker's Name: Unmarked
Marks: None
Origin: U.S.A.
Size: 9¼"
Date: circa 1920-1940
Description: Brown cloth doll with original dress and matching head scarf with a white apron. Doll has a wire frame which enables her to bend. Thread stitched eyes, eyebrows and nose of black, mouth is red stitched. Excellent condition.
Comments: Handmade doll - not uncommon but scarce from this period.
Courtesy of: Angie's Doll Boutique
Price Range: $50.00-65.00

Name: "No Name" Male - Boy
Maker's Name: Unmarked
Marks: None
Origin: U.S.A.
Size: 7¼"
Date: circa 1935-1950
Description: Young boy made of cloth with a wire frame. Black straw hair (dyed) with a straw hat, stitched eyes and mouth. Cotton shirt and overalls. Doll is holding some straw and a stick in his hands. No shoes.
Comments: Souvenir folk-art dolls of this type are common and plentiful.
Courtesy of: Angie's Doll Boutique
Price Range: $25.00-40.00

Name: Golliwog
Maker's Name: Unmarked
Marks: None
Origin: England
Size: 16¼"
Date: circa 1920s-1950s
Description: Black felt body with plastic eyes of white with black plastic pupils, applied nose of felt with applied red felt lips. Dressed in a felt tux with tails, felt tie and vest and cotton pants. Felt feet to simulate shoes. Wool curly hair of light brown. All original. Excellent condition.
Comments: Character created from an English child's story circa 1935. Dolls are common and plentiful (unmarked ones).
Courtesy of: Angie's Doll Boutique
Price Range: $110.00-125.00

Name: "No Name" Male - Boy
Maker's Name: Unmarked
Marks: None
Origin: U.S.A.
Size: 15¾"
Date: circa 1940-1950
Description: Oil cloth brown doll with curly dark brown yarn hair, stitched black eyes with light brown stitched pupils, nose and ears, red stitched mouth. Jointed at the shoulders and hips. Cotton jumpsuit/overalls. All original cotton stuffed body. Original clothing.
Comments: Common doll made from doll kits available during the 1940s and 1950s.
Courtesy of: Angie's Doll Boutique
Price Range: $40.00-75.00

Name: "No Name" Female - Adult
Maker's Name: Unmarked
Marks: None
Origin: U.S.A.
Size: 8½"
Date: circa 1940s
Description: Oil cloth brown doll with original clothing and head scarf. Painted features and original brass earrings. Excellent condition.
Comments: Handmade dolls of this type are common and plentiful.
Courtesy of: Angie's Doll Boutique
Price Range: $40.00-65.00

Name: "No Name" Female - Adult
Maker's Name: Unmarked
Marks: None
Origin: U.S.A.
Size: 8½"
Date: circa 1880-1910
Description: Silk stockinette doll with bold beige stitched features. Straw skirt and hat (lined with features). Shell necklace. All original. Excellent condition.
Comments: Not uncommon but scarce handmade doll.
Courtesy of: Angie's Doll Boutique
Price Range: $145.00-185.00

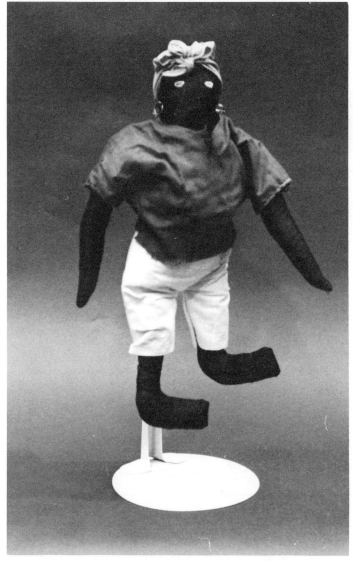

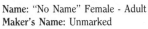

Name: "No Name" Female - Adult
Maker's Name: Unmarked
Marks: None
Origin: U.S.A.
Size: 10¼"
Date: circa 1910-1930
Description: Silk stockinette body with stitched features of silk thread. Original clothing (skirt missing) and brass earrrings. Good condition.
Comments: Handmade, common. Dolls of this time period are becoming scarce.
Courtesy of: Angie's Doll Boutique
Price Range: $95.00-125.00

Name: Topsy-Turvy
Maker's Name: Unmarked
Marks: None
Origin:
Size: 13″
Date: circa 1930-1950
Description: Brown felt and black felt double ended dolls. All applied felt features. Painted wooden necklaces and brass earrings and bracelets. Cotton printed dress and market attire on the black colored doll. Solid dress with mesh blouse on the brown colored doll in party attire. All original. Excellent condition.
Comments: Dolls from the Islands are common but the topsy-turvy types are uncommon.
Courtesy of: Angie's Doll Boutique
Price Range: $135.00-175.00

Name: Little Red Riding Hood
Maker's Name: Frankie Lile
Marks: None
Origin: U.S.A.
Size: 14¾"
Date: circa 1950-1960
Description: Light brown stockinette doll. Young girl with black yarn hair, stitched features, felt shoes and cotton socks. All original.
Comments: Doll is machine stitched with some hand stitching by a modern folk-artist. Dolls made by modern folk-artist are plentiful with the older ones usually costing more.
Courtesy of: Angie's Doll Boutqiue (owner/doll artist)
Price Range: $75.00-100.00

Name: "No Name" Female - Adult
Maker's Name: Unmarked
Marks: None
Origin: U.S.A.
Size: 13"
Date: circa 1880-1910
Description: Silk stockintette doll with stitched silk thread features. Satin dress with matching cap. Hand stitched lace collar and under-pants, leather shoes with satin laces. All original. Excellent condition.
Comments: Well dressed early handmade dolls of good quality as the one described above are scarce. American-made Black cloth dolls of this quality are even scarcer.
Courtesy of: Angie's Doll Boutique
Price Range: $150.00-200.00

Name: "No Name" Female - Adult
Maker's Name: Unmarked
Marks: None
Origin: U.S.A.
Size: 7¼"
Date: circa 1870-1890s
Description: Silk stockinette doll with leather hands displaying separate fingers. Wool hair, stitched eyes and brows with molded nose, lips are red stitched. Clothing is all original, carrying a bundle on her head and a scarf on her neck. Dress and accessories are made of cotton. Excellent condition.
Comments: This doll is of exceptional quality and exhibits detailed features. Scarce.
Courtesy of: Angie's Doll Boutique
Price Range: $175.00-200.00

Name: Vanity Doll Female - Adult
Maker's Name: Unmarked
Marks: None
Origin: U.S.A.
Size: 6¾"
Date: circa 1940-1950
Description: Cloth half-dolls were usually used as toaster covers, but the size of this doll, 6¾" indicates that it may have been used on a vanity table to cover cosmetics. Cloth top-half with button eyes, stitched red nose, mouth and eyebrows, white plastic earrings and black yarn hair, scarf on head, white apron over a print dress. All original.
Comments: These dolls are common and plentiful. The size of this doll makes it unusual. The doll is only 6¾" from the top of the head to the hem-line on the dress.
Courtesy of: Angie's Doll Boutique
Price Range: $75.00-100.00

Name: Mammy-type Female - Adult
Maker's Name: Unmarked
Marks: None
Origin: U.S.A.
Size: 3"
Date: circa 1910-1930s
Description: All cloth black colored doll with original clothing, holding a White 1½" celluloid baby. The cloth of the doll has been stiffened by a glue mixture. Painted features. Good condition.
Comments: Common, but the doll described above is an unusual size (only 3"), also plentiful in larger sizes.
Courtesy of: Angie's Doll Boutique
Price Range: $35.00-60.00

Name: "No Name" Female - Adult
Maker's Name: Unmarked
Marks: None
Origin: U.S.A.
Size: 11″
Date: circa 1930-1950s
Description: Cloth busty adult doll with bold stitches of silk thread forming facial features. Original print dress with matching hat and white apron. Large yellow celluloid earrings. Excellent condition.
Comments: Common and plentiful.
Courtesy of: Angie's Doll Boutique
Price Range: $60.00-85.00

Name: "No Name" Female - Adult
Maker's Name: Unmarked
Marks: None
Origin: U.S.A.
Size: 5¼″
Date: circa 1930-1950
Description: All cloth adult doll with original head scarf, dress not original. Painted features. Fair condition.
Comments: Common and plentiful.
Courtesy of: Angie's Doll Boutique
Price Range: $35.00-50.00 (all original)

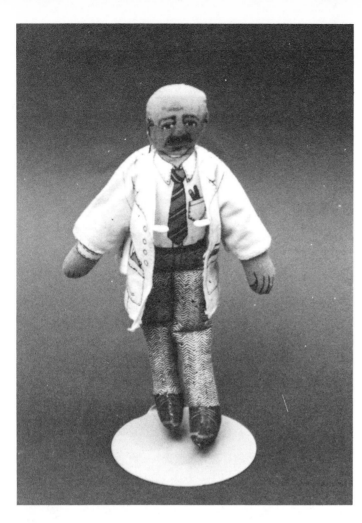

Name: George Washington Carver Male - Adult
Maker's Name: Hallmark Cards, Inc.
Marks: Hallmark Cards, Inc. K.C. Mo. 64141. Made in Taiwan
Origin: Taiwan / Sold in America
Size: 7¼″
Date: circa 1970
Description: All cloth male doll with lithographed features and shirt/shoes, cotton laboratory coat and pants. Good condition.
Comments: Historical Blacks in America were created in doll-form by many companies during the late 1960s-1970s.
Courtesy of: Angie's Doll Boutique
Price Range: $25.00-55.00

Name: "No Name" Female - Adult
Maker's Name: Unmarked
Marks: None
Origin: U.S.A.
Size: 10¼″
Date: circa 1940s-1950s
Description: Matronly adult doll made of black cloth with painted features (mouth open with white paint for teeth), gray yarn tuffs for hair, gold earring, all original clothing and head kerchief. Body of the doll is flat instead of full-shaped. Excellent condition.
Comments: Dolls of the above type are common and usually plentiful.
Courtesy of: Davern Collection
Price Range: $70.00-95.00

Name: Topsy-Turvy Female - Adults   **Courtesy of:** Davern Collection
Maker's Name: Unmarked   **Price Range:** $85.00-125.00
Marks: None
Origin: U.S.A.
Size: 14½"
Date: circa 1920s-1940s
Description: All cloth double-ended doll with a Black female on one end and a White
    female on the other end. Both females are attired in long dresses made of cloth
    and the Black doll wears a head kerchief. White doll has yarn hair. Each doll
    has stitched silk thread features. All original. Excellent condition.
Comments: Topsy-Turvy dolls are common from the above time period and plentiful.

Name: "No Name" Female - Adult
Maker's Name: Unmarked
Marks: None
Origin: U.S.A.
Size: 7"
Date: circa 1930-1940s
Description: Black satin body doll with button eyes, stitched nostrils and mouth. Body
    of the doll is terminated in a flat round shape (no feet). Original silk dress with
    matching head kerchief and a silk white shawl and apron. Excellent condition.
Comments: Unusual size and materials which the doll is made of and dressed in. The
    type of doll however, is common.
Courtesy of: Davern Collection
Price Range: $65.00-85.00

Name: Flip Wilson / Geraldine
Maker's Name: Operation Bootstraps, Inc.
Origin: U.S.A.
Size: 17″
Date: circa 1970
Description: Cloth, lithographed double-sided doll of a male and a female in the image of Flip Wilson, a TV comedian. A pull-string activates voice. Good condition.
Comments: Operation Bootstraps was an organization formed to aid in self-motivation among minorities during the 1970s.
Courtesy of: Davern Collection
Price Range: $25.00-45.00

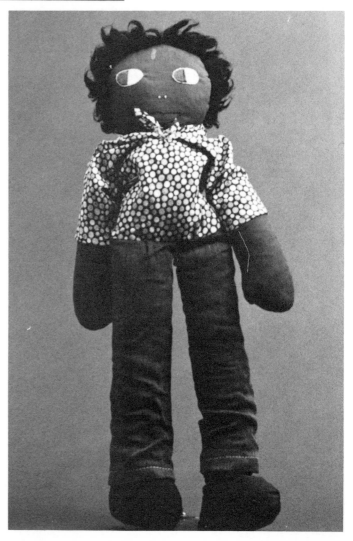

Name: Golliwog
Maker's Name: Unmarked
Marks: None
Origin: U.S.A.
Size: 19¼″
Date: circa 1950s
Description: Medium brown male doll made in the image of a Golliwog character in an English storybook. Applied eyes, stitched nostrils and mouth, mohair wig. Clothing original and attached to the body at various points, lithographed shoes (attached to feet), ascot on neck. Very good condition.
Comments: Homecrafted Golliwogs are not common, but they are available.
Courtesy of: Davern Collection
Price Range: $75.00-95.00

Name: Andy
Maker's Name: Unmarked
Marks: None
Origin: U.S.A.
Size: 16″
Date: circa 1960s
Description: Character from the Raggety Ann play/musical, Andy. Homecrafted with brown cloth body, orange yarn hair, original clothing, lithographed legs and shoes, stitched features with button eyes. Excellent condition.
Comments: Homecrafted Black Andy & Ann dolls are not common but they are available.
Courtesy of: Davern Collection
Price Range: $40.00-65.00

Name: "No Name" Female - Adult
Maker's Name: Unmarked
Marks: None
Origin: U.S.A.
Size: 10″
Date: circa 1930s
Description: Cloth adult doll, black with painted features. All original clothing, busty chest and head kerchief. Very good condition.
Comments: Common and plentiful.
Courtesy of: Davern Collection
Price Range: $45.00-65.00

Name: Topsy-Turvy
Maker's Name: Unmarked
Marks: None
Origin: U.S.A.
Size: 9½"
Date: circa 1940s-1950s
Description: Tubular shaped felt double-ended doll. Black doll has brown mohair tuft on head, felt bonnet. White doll has blonde tuft of mohair, felt bonnet. All original print dress. Painted features. Very good condition.
Comments: Unusual doll-shape and common doll-type. Available.
Courtesy of: Davern Collection
Price Range: $40.00-60.00

Name: Norah Wellings Female - Girl
Maker's Name: Victoria Toy Works
Marks: Norah Wellings / Victoria Toy Works Wellington, Shropshire, England
Origin: England
Size: 18"
Date: circa 1926-1960
Description: All felt creation with felt pants with straps. Stitched fingers and toes (not detailed). Molded face with glass inset eyes, painted red lips and white teeth. Mohair wig. Good condition.
Comments: Norah Wellings' dolls were produced until the early 1960s. The earlier dolls have felt faces and the later ones may be found with thin plastic face-masks (1950s-1960s)/composition face-masks (1930s-1940s).
Courtesy of: Yesteryear's Museum
Price Range: $165.00-195.00

Name: Norah Wellings Female - Girl
Maker's Name: Norah Wellings
Marks: None
Origin: England
Size: 18"
Date: circa 1926-1960
Description: All felt girl dressed in a grass skirt and felt lei around her neck, ties on her wrist, bands on her ankles. Glass inset eyes, molded face, painted lips and teeth, mohair wig. Excellent condition.
Comments: Norah Wellings dolls are usually marked but when unmarked, the trained eye can detect the Wellings trademark of stylization and materials used.
Courtesy of: Yesteryear's Museum
Price Range: $150.00-175.00 (unmarked)

Name: Norah Wellings Male - Adult
Maker's Name: Norah Wellings
Marks: None
Origin: England
Size: 19½"
Date: circa 1926-1960s
Description: All felt male doll with molded face, inset glass eyes, painted red lips and white teeth. Original clothing (not attached to the doll), denim overalls, cotton shirt with gauze bow-tie. Stitched fingers and molded feet (shoe-shaped). Mohair wig under a straw hat. Excellent condition.
Comments: Norah Wellings male dolls are scarce.
Courtesy of: Yesteryear's Museum
Price Range: $195.00-300.00

Name: Aunt Jemima, Uncle Mose, Wade and Diana
Maker's Name: Unmarked
Marks: Each character's name is on the back of the dolls
Origin: U.S.A.
Size: Mother 13¾"; Father 14¾"; Son 11¾" and Daughter 10½"
Date: circa 1920s-1930s
Description: All cloth lithographed family. Colorful cloth with the legs of the father, son and daughter freely attached, Aunt Jemima doll legs are not visible under her long dress. All dolls are in excellent condition.
Comments: Early cloth doll families as described above are scarce. These dolls were sold as patterns and made by individuals.
Courtesy of: Yesteryear's Museum
Price Range: $300.00-375.00 set

Name: "WPA" (Works Project Administration) Doll
Maker's Name: Handi Craft Project / Milwaukee State Teachers College
Marks: (left foot): U.S.A. Handi Craft Project, Sponsor: Milwaukee State Teachers College
Origin: U.S.A.
Size: 22½"
Date: circa 1930s
Description: Cloth body colored brown and stiffened texture, black yarn hair, molded painted features, stitched fingers and toes, original shoes - clothing not original. Excellent condition.
Comments: The Works Project Administration (WPA) was developed during the 1930s and early 40s as an effort to put Black artists to work. Artwork made as a direct result of the above project is scarce but available.
Courtesy of: Angie's Doll Boutique
Price Range: $650.00-850.00 (all original warrants the highest figure)

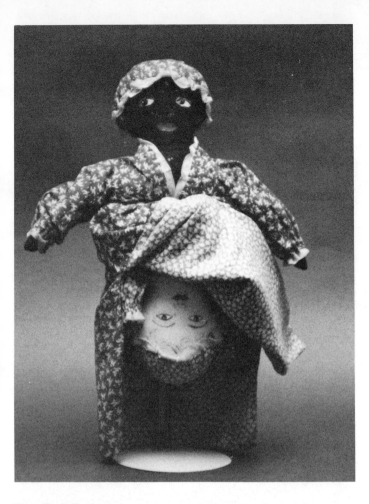

Name: Topsy Turvy
Maker's Name: Unmarked
Marks: None
Origin: U.S.A.
Size: 13"
Date: circa 1930-1940s
Description: All cloth double headed doll. Black doll head dressed in red print long
    sleeve dress with a matching bonnet on her head. White doll head with a blue
    identical outfit. Both heads have painted features. Excellent condition.
Comments: Plentiful and available.
Courtesy of: Yesteryear's Museum
Price Range: $90.00-125.00

Name: "No Name" Female - Baby
Maker's Name: Dianne Dengel
Marks: Unmarked
Origin: U.S.A.
Size: 12"
Date: circa 1965-1970
Description: All felt doll with molded painted features, felt hair. Excellent condition.
Comments: Available.
Courtesy of: Yesteryear's Museum
Price Range: $90.00-130.00

Name: Norah Wellings' "Islander" Female - Girl
Maker's Name: Norah Wellings
Marks: Norah Wellings / Made in England
Origin: England
Size: 9"
Date: circa 1926-1960
Description: All felt doll with a black mohair wig, brown body, painted molded features.
    Excellent condition.
Comments: Available.
Courtesy of: Yesteryear's Museum
Price Range: $125.00-135.00

Name: "No Name" Female - Adult
Maker's Name: Unmarked
Marks: None
Origin: U.S.A.
Size: 23"
Date: circa 1930-1950s
Description: All original girl made of brown cloth, stuffed tightly. Painted molded features, brass earrings, brass necklace and bracelet. Curly wool hair, cotton dress, cotton stockings, matching large bow on head with original leather shoes. Excellent condition.
Comments: Scarce.
Courtesy of: Yesteryear's Museum
Price Range: $175.00-245.00

Name: "No Name" Female - Girl
Maker's Name: Unmarked
Marks: None
Origin: U.S.A.
Size: 11½"
Date: circa 1900-1910
Description: Brown cloth body of a young girl with a lithographed molded face mask. Mohair wig. Painted teeth. All original. Excellent condition.
Comments: Common and available.
Courtesy of: Yesteryear's Museum
Price Range: $95.00-125.00

Name: Mammy Liza
Maker's Name: Lillian Warfield, designer / Julia Marie Arnold, Artisan
Marks: Lillian Warfield designer circa 1930 pattern / Julia Marie Arnold Artisan Mississippi
Origin: U.S.A. (Mississippi)
Size: 15″ lady; 2½″ baby
Date: circa 1930-1970
Description: Coarse, cloth brown cotton stuffed adult doll, embroidered features, gray wool curly hair, brass hoop earrings, yellow good luck beads. Adult doll is holding small White baby made of celluloid, dressed in white cotton gown and cap.
Comments: The doll described above is an early example circa 1930s. The earlier dolls are valued higher because of their age. All of the dolls made by Julia Marie Arnold are considered collectible.
Price Range: $165.00-220.00

Name: "No Name" Female - Adult
Maker's Name: Unmarked
Marks: None
Origin: U.S.A.
Size: 14½″
Date: circa 1940s
Description: All cloth cotton stuffed doll. All original clothing, stitched features, mitten fingers with thumb on each hand.
Comments: Available and plentiful.
Price Range: $90.00-125.00

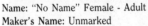

Name: "No Name" Female - Adult
Maker's Name: Unmarked
Marks: None
Origin: U.S.A.
Size: 12″
Date: circa 1940s
Description: All cloth doll with embroidered features and applied nose. Original clothing. Excellent condition.
Comments: Available and plentiful.
Price Range: $95.00-125.00

141

Name: Aunt Jemima type
Maker's Name: Unmarked
Marks: None
Origin: U.S.A.
Size: 12½″
Date: circa 1900-1930s
Description: Oil cloth black doll with painted features, brass earrings, original clothing. Good condition.
Comments: Plentiful.
Courtesy of: Charlene Upham
Price Range: $65.00-90.00

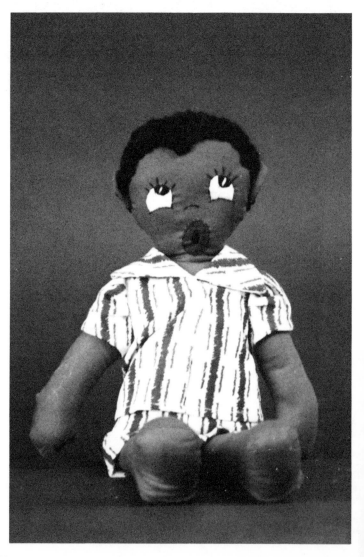

Name: "No Name" Male - Boy
Maker's Name: Unmarked
Marks: None
Origin: U.S.A.
Size: 16¾″
Date: circa 1940-1950s
Description: All cloth young boy dressed in his original short pant suit. Embroidered features with short curly wool hair and applied ears. Excellent condition.
Comments: Male dolls are usually scarcer than female dolls. The doll described above is available but not plentiful.
Price Range: $75.00-90.00

Name: Golliwog "Mr. Golly"
Maker's Name: Dean's Child Toys LTD.
Marks: Dean's (Mr. Golly) Rag Book Co. LTD. London England (on left foot)
Origin: England
Size: 13″
Date: circa 1970 to present
Description: Lithographed cloth stuffed doll. Large heart-shaped card in vest coat. Short straight grayish/black wig. Excellent condition.
Comments: The above dolls are being made today and they are representative of the 1930s version.
Price Range: $55.00-75.00

Name: Mammy-type with baby
Maker's Name: Unmarked
Marks: None
Origin: U.S.A.
Size: 13½″ adult; 2½″ baby
Date: circa 1930s
Description: All cloth doll with a small celluloid White doll dressed in a long cotton gown. Both dolls are in original clothing. The adult doll has embroidered features and button eyes with brass earrings. Excellent condition.
Comments: Available
Price Range: $95.00-125.00

143

Name: "No Name" Female - Girl
Maker's Name: Unmarked
Marks: None
Origin: U.S.A.
Size: 16"
Date: circa 1940-1950s
Description: All cloth doll in the image of a young girl with stitched features and black yarn
     hair. Original clothing and white cotton stockings. Shoes missing. Good condition.
Comments: Available
Courtesy of: Davern Collection
Price Range: $55.00-85.00

Name: "No Name" Female - Girl
Maker's Name: Unmarked
Marks: None
Origin: U.S.A.
Size: 16¼"
Date: circa 1930s-1950s
Description: All cloth doll with black yarn hair. Original clothing. Embroidered
    features. Excellent condition.
Comments: Available
Courtesy of: Davern Collection
Price Range: $65.00-85.00

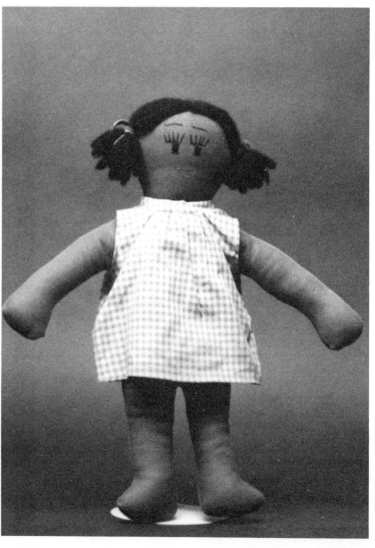

Name: "No Name" Female - Adult
Maker's Name: Unmarked
Marks: None
Origin: U.S.A.
Size: 6″
Date: circa 1930-1940s
Description: Bust of a female adult used as a pin cushion. Felt upper body with felt applied features and felt hat, mohair wig with brass earrings. Excellent condition.
Comments: Available
Courtesy of: Davern Collection
Price Range: $45.00-65.00

Name: Jean
Maker's Name: Unmarked
Marks: "Jean" painted on the shawl
Origin: U.S.A.
Size: 11″
Date: circa 1920-1930s
Description: Stockinette cloth body with black yarn hair. Original cotton dress with a shawl and brass earrings. Painted features with mitt hands. All original. Excellent condition.
Comments: Available but not plentiful.
Courtesy of: Davern Collection
Price Range: $125.00-150.00

Name: "No Name" Female - Young Adult
Maker's Name: Unmarked
Marks: None
Origin: U.S.A.
Size: 12½″
Date: circa 1930-1940s
Description: Dark brown doll with cloth body and stitched features, mitt hands. All original clothing. Unusual stitched smiling face with teeth. Excellent condition.
Comments: Extremely well made doll with a charming face made of cloth, a highly sought after collectible.
Courtesy of: Davern Collection
Price Range: $120.00-150.00

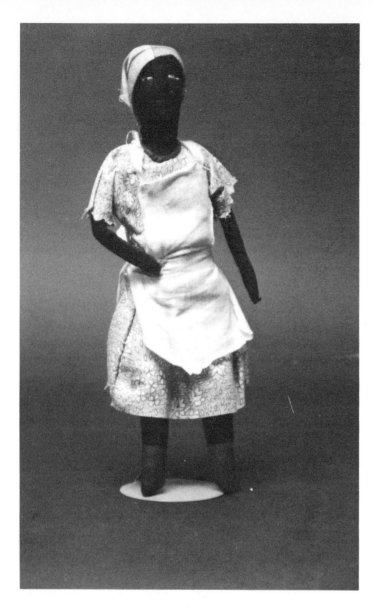

Name: "No Name" Female - Adult
Maker's Name: Unmarked
Marks: None
Origin: U.S.A.
Size: 12″
Date: circa 1920-1940s
Description: All cloth adult doll with stitched features and original clothing. Shoes are sewn and function as feet terminating in a shoe-shape (red). Good condition.
Comments: Available but not plentiful.
Courtesy of: Davern Collection
Price Range: $70.00-125.00

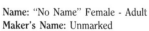

Name: "No Name" Female - Adult
Maker's Name: Unmarked
Marks: None
Origin: U.S.A.
Size: 11″
Date: circa 1920-1940s
Description: All cloth doll with stitched features in the image of an older Black lady. Hair is grayish/white yarn. Original clothing. Excellent condition.
Comments: Available but not plentiful.
Courtesy of: Davern Collection
Price Range: $65.00-95.00

Name: "No Name" Female - Adult
Maker's Name: Unmarked
Marks: None
Origin: U.S.A.
Size: 10⅝"
Date: circa 1930-1940s
Description: All cloth adult female doll with stitched features and brass earrings. Original clothing. Button eyes. Excellent condition.
Comments: Available and plentiful.
Courtesy of: Davern Collection
Price Range: $50.00-75.00

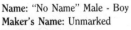

Name: "No Name" Male - Boy
Maker's Name: Unmarked
Marks: None
Origin: U.S.A.
Size: 10½"
Date: circa 1920-1940s
Description: All cloth doll with stitched features. The doll is made in the image of a young boy wearing his original cotton overalls, ascot and hat with color coordinated shirt. Excellent condition.
Comments: Male dolls are scarce and Black male dolls are scarce and highly sought after.
Courtesy of: Davern Collection
Price Range: $85.00-100.00

Name: "No Name" Male - Boy
Maker's Name: Unmarked
Marks: None
Origin: Jamaica
Size: 11⅜"
Date: circa 1940-1950s
Description: All cloth male doll with painted features and original clothing with straw hat.
Comments: Available and plentiful.
Courtesy of: Davern Collection
Price Range: $50.00-85.00

Name: "No Name" Female - Girl
Maker's Name: Unmarked
Marks: None
Origin: U.S.A.
Size: 7¾"
Date: circa 1930-1940s
Description: Stockinette girl doll with a mohair wig and stitch-
        ed fetures. Orignal clothing. Excellent condition.
Comments: Common but scarce in sizes as small as the one
        above.
Courtesy of: Davern Collection
Price Range: $60.00-95.00

Name: "No Name" Female - girl
Maker's Name: Unmarked
Marks: None
Origin: U.S.A.
Size: 8¾"
Date: circa 1930-1950s
Description: All felt doll with applied features, ties on wrists and ankles. Original felt dress. Excellent condition.
Comments: Common and available.
Courtesy of: Davern Collection
Price Range: $50.00-75.00

Name: "No Name" Couple/girl and boy
Maker's Name: Unmarked
Marks: None
Origin: U.S.A.
Size: 12¼"
Date: circa 1930s-1950s
Description: All cloth light brown children with full black yarn wigs and original clothing. Stitched features, lines drawn on feet and hands to represent toes and fingers. Each doll has exaggerated features. Good condition.
Comments: Not scarce as singles but pairs of rag dolls are scarce. Earlier pairs are very rare (prior to 1900).
Courtesy of: Davern Collection
Price Range: $80.00-100.00 pair

Name: "No Name" Female - Girl
Maker's Name: Unmarked
Marks: None
Origin: U.S.A.
Size: 11½"
Date: circa 1900-1930s
Description: Stockinette doll stuffed with cotton. Stitched features with button eyes. Feet are tied with yarn at the ankles. Black yarn hair. Original clothing. Good condition.
Comments: Available but not plentiful in the style described above.
Courtesy of: Nancy Saad
Price Range: $75.00-100.00

Name: "No Name" Female - Adult
Maker's Name: Unmarked
Marks: None
Origin: U.S.A.
Size: 13¾"
Date: circa 1900-1920s
Description: Tightly molded stuffed cloth body with a molded mask-face. Painted features. Black yarn hair in braids. Original clothing with satin shoes, cotton print dress, ruffled sleeves, white apron and matching bonnet. Excellent condition.
Comments: Well dressed doll available but not plentiful.
Courtesy of: Yarmouth County Museum
Price Range: $250.00-300.00

Name: "No Name" Female - Adult
Maker's Name: Unmarked
Marks: None
Origin: Trinidad
Size: 11"
Date: circa 1902
Description: All cloth doll representative of a market place woman carrying her wares in a tray atop her head. The doll is handmade of a black mercerised cotton with stitched eyes and mouth with an applied nose of the same fabric. Mitt hands and shaped feet. All original clothing and head-wrap. Hair made of black silk thread. Excellent condition.
Comments: Scarce from the early 20th century. Later dolls are easier to obtain.
Courtesy of: Yarmouth County Museum
Price Range: $195.00-250.00

Name: "No Name" Male - Adult
Maker's Name: Unmarked
Marks: None
Origin: Bahamas
Size: 15"
Date: circa 1940s-1950s
Description: Brown cloth male doll with painted eyes, nose and mouth with a grass beard (dyed black). Original clothing, hat and sandals. Excellent condition.
Comments: Available and plentiful.
Price Range: $65.00-90.00

Name: "No Name" Female - Adult
Maker's Name: Unmarked
Marks: None
Origin: U.S.A.
Size: 17"
Date: circa 1900-1920s
Description: Brown tightly sewn cloth body with stitched features. All original with one earring and matching ornament attached to the shawl. Excellent condition.
Comments: Doll has a West Indies style but the cloth used is typical of an American doll. The stitched hands also indicate that the doll is indeed American.
Price Range: $195.00-225.00

Name: "No Name" Male - Boy
Maker's Name: Unmarked
Marks: None
Origin: U.S.A.
Size: 8½"
Date: circa 1930s-1940s
Description: Light brown male doll with a flat body and stitched features. All original clothing with fleeced sewn black wig. Excellent condition.
Comments: Male dolls are scarce made prior to 1900. After 1920s, male dolls are available but not plentiful.
Courtesy of: Angie's Doll Boutique
Price Range: $80.00-100.00

Name: No-Name
Maker's Name: Unmarked
Marks: None
Origin: U.S.A.
Size: 4½″
Date: circa 1910-1930s
Description: Delicately executed cloth doll with painted
    molded features, mohair wig, black sewn boots.
    Original clothing. Excellent condition.
Comments: Common style but dolls less than 5″ that are
    well executed in cloth are **rare**.
Courtesy of: Ron Carr Collection
Price Range: $90.00-110.00

Name: No-Name
Maker's Name: California
Marks: California
Origin: California
Size: 6½″ each
Date: circa 1930s-1950s
Description: Brown stockinette dolls, cotton stuffed with stitched features and black
    yarn hair. Original clothing. Excellent condition.
Comments: Common.
Courtesy of: M. Davern Collection
Price Range: $85.00-120.00 (pair)

Name: No-Name
Maker's Name: Unmarked
Marks: None
Origin: U.S.A.
Size: 12″
Date: circa 1940s-1950s
Description: Cloth dolls with curly yarn hair, cloth applied eyes, stitched mouths.
    Original clothing (well dressed). Excellent condition.
Comments: Common.
Courtesy of: M. Davern Collection
Price Range: $125.00-160.00 (pair)

Name: No-Name
Maker's Name: Unmarked
Marks: None
Origin: U.S.A.
Size: 15¾"
Date: 1900-1920s
Description: Cloth medium brown doll with stitched features, black yarn hair, with wooden arms and legs. Original clothing. Excellent condition.
Comments: Common but unusual for 20th century cloth dolls to have wooden legs and arms.
Courtesy of: M. Davern Collection
Price Range: $110.00-175.00

Name: No-Name
Maker's Name: Unmarked
Marks: None
Origin: U.S.A.
Size: 16¼"
Date: circa 1950-1965
Description: All cloth dolls with black yarn hair, stitched and applied features. Original clothing. Medium brown coloring. Excellent condition.
Comments: Common.
Courtesy of: M. Davern Collection
Price Range: $95.00-125.00 (pair)

Name: No-Name
Maker's Name: Unmarked
Marks: None
Origin: U.S.A.
Size: 6½″
Date: circa 1930-1950
Description: All-cloth greyish black doll with stitched features. Original clothing. Good condition.
Comments: Common.
Courtesy of: M. Davern Collection
Price Range: $40.00-65.00

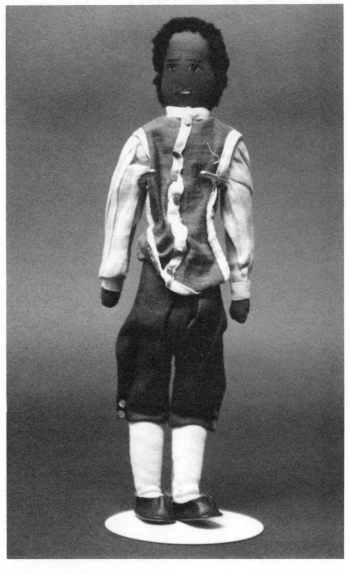

Name: No-Name
Maker's Name: Unmarked
Marks: None
Origin: U.S.A.
Size: 14¼″
Date: circa 1930-1950
Description: All cloth brown male with leather shoes and all original clothing (well dressed). Black curly yarn hair with stitched features. Excellent condition.
Comments: Scarce.
Courtesy of: M. Davern Collection
Price Range: $80.00-110.00

Name: No-Name
Maker's Name: Unmarked
Marks: None
Origin: U.S.A.
Size: 17½″ (male), 19″ (female)
Date: circa 1935-1945
Description: Brown cloth dolls with stitched features and black yarn hair.
Comments: Plentiful.
Courtesy of: M. Davern Collection
Price Range: $90.00-110.00 (pair)

Name: No-Name
Maker's Name: Unmarked
Marks: None
Origin: U.S.A.
Size: 15¾″
Date: circa 1920-1940
Description: All cloth adult female doll. Black with stitched features, straw hat and handbag. Original clothing. Excellent condition.
Comments: Common.
Courtesy of: M. Davern Collection
Price Range: $95.00-125.00

156

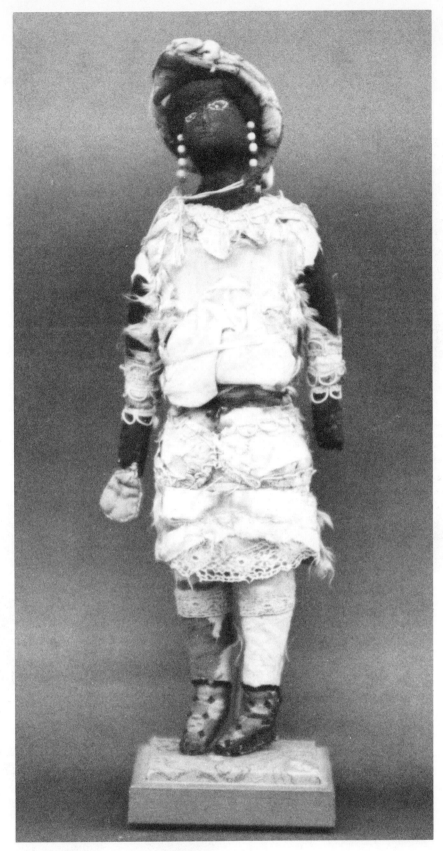

Name: No-Name
Maker's Name: Unmarked
Marks: None
Origin: U.S.A.
Size: 15¼"
Date: circa 1920s

Comments: Scarce.
Courtesy of: Charlene Upham Antiques, Mardela Springs, Maryland
Price Range: $225.00-300.00

Description: Stockinette black adult doll. Silk and lace clothing. Molded and stitched features. Only remnants of the dress and lacy undergarments remain (original), with original leather boots. The doll's body is in excellent condition.

Name: No-Name
Maker's Name: Unmarked
Marks: None
Origin: U.S.A.
Size: 11¼"
Date: circa 1920-1945
Description: Stockinette male black doll with the fabric stretched over a rolled newspaper. Original clothing. Stitched mouth and nose with buttons attached for the eyes. Excellent condition.
Comments: Scarce.
Courtesy of: M. Davern Collection
Price Range: $70.00-100.00

Name: No-Name
Maker's Name: Unmarked
Marks: None
Origin: U.S.A.
Size: 19½"
Date: circa 1900-1930s
Description: Brown cloth stockinette doll with stitched features. Original leather boots, redressed. Black yarn hair. Fair condition.
Comments: Common.
Courtesy of: Charlene Upham Antiques, Mardela Springs, Maryland
Price Range: $165.00-275.00 (higher price - excellent condition)

Name: No-Name
Maker's Name: Unmarked
Marks: None
Origin: U.S.A.
Size: 13½″
Date: circa 1900-1930
Description: Black cloth doll with jointed legs, each finger is well articulated with red sewn fingernails, black yarn hair, stitched eyes. Original clothing and shoes (boots). Excellent condition.
Comments: Scarce.
Courtesy of: Charlene Upham Antiques, Mardela Springs, Maryland
Price Range: $150.00-225.00

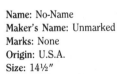

Name: No-Name
Maker's Name: Unmarked
Marks: None
Origin: U.S.A.
Size: 14½″
Date: circa 1900-1930s
Description: Black cloth doll with curly black hair and blue eyes. Stitched features, sewn cloth boots. Original satin dress. Excellent condition.
Comments: Common.
Courtesy of: Charlene Upham Antiques, Mardela Springs, Maryland
Price Range: $125.00-165.00

Composition and

Papier Mache Dolls

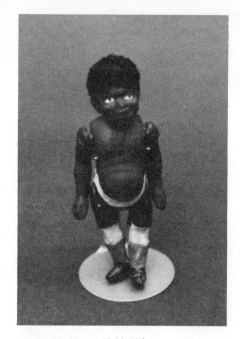

Name: "No Name" Child (Male)
Maker's Name: Unmarked
Marks: None
Origin: Germany
Size: 4¼"
Date: circa 1880-1910
Description: Rough papier mache doll representing a male child. Painted boots and lower torso, wool wig, brown painted eyes, red lips, jointed arms and legs. Good condition.
Comments: Exaggerated features.
Courtesy of: Angie's Doll Boutique
Price Range: $125.00-185.00

Name: Tony Sarge "Marionette"
Maker's Name: Unmarked
Marks: None
Origin: U.S.A.
Size: 11½"
Date: circa 1920s-1940s
Description: Dark brown composition male marionette with exaggerated, painted features, smiling face with painted teeth, molded fingers and feet, fully jointed. All original clothing and soft black straight mohair wig. Dressed in suspender-pants and long sleeve blouse. Excellent condition.
Comments: Available but not plentiful.
Courtesy of: Silver Springs "Museum"
Price Range: $275.00-350.00

Name: "No Name" Female - Adult
Maker's Name: Unmarked
Marks: None
Origin: U.S.A.
Size: 13½"
Date: circa 1930s-1940s
Description: Light brown composition female representing an adult with a toddler's body. Fully jointed, molded painted features, gray wool hair under a head kerchief, long cotton plaid dress with shoes and cotton stockings. All original. Excellent condition.
Comments: Available and plentiful.
Courtesy of: Silver Springs "Museum"
Price Range: $90.00-135.00

Name: Check An' Double Check "Amos" **Courtesy of:** Silver Springs "Museum"
Maker's Name: Unmarked **Price Range:** $195.00-225.00
Marks: CHECK AN' DOUBLE CHECK AMOS
Origin: U.S.A.
Size: 11″ - 15″
Date: circa 1920s-1940s
Description: Dark brown composition head, arms and legs. Cloth stuffed body. All
   original clothing with original tag. Painted features/molded. Doll is wearing
   checkered long black/white pants with matching shawl (suspenders) and a mat-
   ching cap with a bib. Excellent condition.
Comments: Part of a 3 doll series representing the Amos and Andy characters from
   the Columbia Broadcasting System. Available but not plentiful.

Name: Check An' Double Check "Andy"
Maker's Name: Unmarked
Marks: CHECK AN' DOUBLE CHECK ANDY (on a diamond shaped card)
Origin: U.S.A.
Size: 11″ - 15″
Date: circa 1920s-1940s
Description: Dark brown composition doll fully clothed (all original). Painted features,
   composition arms, head and legs, cloth body. Excellent condition. Molded tinted
   hair.
Comments: Doll has original name tag on his clothing. There are 3 dolls in this series:
   Andy, Amos and Madam Queen. *Dolls represent the characters from the Amos
   and Andy Show on the Columbia Broadcasting System. Available but not plentiful.
Courtesy of: Silver Springs "Museum"
Price Range: $195.00-225.00

Name: Check An' Double Check " Madam Queen"
Maker's Name: Unmarked
Marks: CHECK AN' DOUBLE CHECK Madam Queen
Origin: U.S.A.
Size: 11″ - 15″
Date: circa 1920s-1940s
Description: Dark brown composition head, arms and legs with a cotton stuffed body.
   Painted features with molded nose and mouth. All original clothing and hat with
   molded tinted hair. Excellent condition.
Comments: Original name tag on clothing. Part of a 3 doll series: Amos, Andy and
   Madam Queen representing characters from the Amos and Andy Show on the
   Columbia Broadcasting System. Available but not plentiful.
Courtesy of: Silver Springs "Museum"
Price Range: $195.00-225.00

Name: Topsy-type
Maker's Name: Unmarked
Marks: None
Origin: U.S.A.
Size: 9″
Date: circa 1920s-1940s
Description: Brown all-composition toddler body, with molded painted features, painted molded hair with 3 hair tufts, fully jointed. All original. Excellent condition.
Comments: Available and plentiful.
Courtesy of: Dolly Wares Doll Museum
Price Range: $100.00-140.00

Name: "No Name" Male - Boy
Maker's Name: Unmarked
Marks: None
Origin: Fiji Islands
Size: 9″
Date: circa 1890s-1910
Description: All composition in a rough texture, fully jointed, molded strong ethnic features, *molded chest muscles, painted eyes and fleeced black curly hair (short). Original brass earrings and fur skirt. Excellent condition.
Comments: Scarce.
Courtesy of: Dolly Wares Doll Museum
Price Range: $195.00-230.00

Name: Rufus Rastus Johnson Brown
Maker's Name: Unmarked
Marks: None
Origin: U.S.A.
Size: 21″
Date: circa 1920s-1930s
Description: Composition brown head with a tight molded cloth body. Character portrays a Black musician of the era who recorded on the "Victor" label. The doll has exaggerated features enhanced by white paint. A fiddle and "real" 78 album came with the doll. All original. Excellent condition.
Comments: Rare as a complete set. Scarce, even as an incomplete set.
Courtesy of: Dolly Wares Doll Museum
Price Range: $275.00-350.00

Name: "No Name" Male - Adult
Maker's Name: Unmarked
Marks: None
Origin: Cuba
Size: 4″
Date: circa 1900-1920s
Description: Brown composition head, hands and feet. Molded, painted features, open mouth with painted teeth. Fleeced black curly hair. All original clothing and brass earrings. Excellent condition. Crude composition character moves when wound-up/original key.
Comments: Scarce but available.
Courtesy of: Dolly Wares Doll Museum
Price Range: $190.00-250.00

Information for non-black dolls not available.

Name: Famlee Doll
Maker's Name: Change O' Doll Co.
Marks: (original box) Change O' Doll Co.
Origin: U.S.A.
Size: 12″
Date: circa 1926
Description: Composition head doll with changeable screw in heads which include a black composition head. Well dressed doll with Black head boasting a turban, painted eyes, molded mouth and nose. Original box (8 heads total). Excellent condition.
Comments: Scarce.
Courtesy of: Dolly Wares Doll Museum
Price Range: $600.00-750.00

Name: "No Name" Female Adult & Child
Maker's Name: Unmarked
Marks: None
Origin: U.S.A.
Size: 19″
Date: circa 1870
Description: Black papier-mache shoulder head, black glass pupiless inset eyes, closed mouth, black fleecy mohair wig, straw filled brown muslin body, papier-mache lower arms and legs, painted high red boots with blue trim. The adult doll described above is holding an all original miniature black papier-mache doll with black glass inset eyes, wearing painted boots and calico dress. The adult doll is dressed in a calico dress with white apron. Both dolls are made of rough textured papier-mache. Both in excellent condition.
Comments: The dolls described above are excellent examples of Black naturalistic dolls of the 19th century. Scarce as a pair.
Courtesy of: Theriaults
Price Range: $750.00-950.00 pair

165

Information for non-black dolls not available.

Name: "No Name" Male - Baby
Maker's Name: Unmarked
Marks: None
Origin: U.S.A.
Size: 12″
Date: circa 1900-1915
Description: Early dark brown socket head boy on a very tight muslin body, flanged neck, tinted black baby hair and brows, side glancing brown painted eyes, accented nostrils, closed mouth, smiling expression and original short overalls with suspenders and original red shirt. Excellent condition.
Comments: The above doll described, attributed to E.I. Horsman is an excellent example of an early American made composition doll. E.I. Horsmam is now Horsman Dolls, Inc. and at this writing they were celebrating their 125th Anniversary, founded circa 1865.
Courtesy of: Theriaults
Price Range: $195.00-240.00

Name: "No Name" Female - Adult
Maker's Name: Tony Sarge
Marks: None
Origin: U.S.A.
Size: 17″
Date: circa 1940
Description: Brown composition head with flanged neck, painted facial features, brown squinting eyes with large black pupils and white eye dots, heavy molded eyelids, single stroke black brows, broad molded nose, open/closed mouth in wide smiling expression with row of painted teeth, brunette fleeced hair, brown muslin straw filled body, composition lower arms, large hands, molded large brown shoes, original red cotton costume with bandana, white shawl and apron. Very good condition.
Comments: Tony Sarge designed the doll described above for George Borgfeldt, who distributed the doll. Dolls of this type usually held small white celluloid dolls in their arms or they pushed baby carriages with the infant inside. Available but not plentiful.
Courtesy of: Theriaults
Price Range: $375.00 (accessories missing)
$600.00 (complete and original)

Name: "No Name" Female - Toddler
Maker's Name: Unmarked
Marks: None
Origin: U.S.A.
Size: 10″
Date: circa 1930
Description: All brown composition fully jointed doll with painted features, deeply curled tinted hair (molded), chubby toddler body. (Redressed). Excellent condition.
Comments: Common and plentiful. Varying sizes.
Courtesy of: Angie's Doll Boutique
Price Range: $75.00-100.00

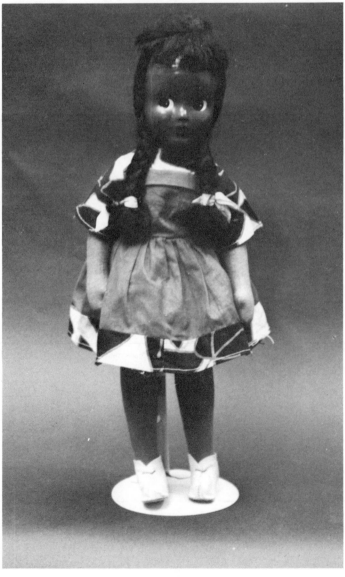

Name: "No Name" Female - Girl
Maker's Name: England (no company name)
Marks: England (left foot)
Origin: England
Size: 15½″
Date: circa 1930s-1940s
Description: Brown composition head on a tight-jointed body made of brown cloth, painted features, mohair braided wig, original clothing and shoes. Excellent condition.
Comments: Typical style of a "Poland" doll made during the same period. Rare doll in the image of a Black child. The status of this doll is scarce but available.
Courtesy of: Angie's Doll Boutqiue
Price Range: $75.00-100.00

Name: "No Name" Female - Girls (2 versions)
Maker's Name: Jamaica (no company name)
Marks: None
Origin: Jamaica
Size: 12"
Date: circa 1930s-1940s
Description: Composition head with a stuffed cloth body, painted features, original outfit. Excellent condition.
Comments: Common and available.
Courtesy of: Angie's Doll Boutique
Price Range: $70.00-90.00

Name: Norah Wellings
Maker's Name: Norah Wellings (Attributed to)
Marks: None
Origin: England
Size: 9½″
Date: circa 1930s-1940s
Description: Dark brown composition female head on a felt plush child's body, painted features, wool hair, original lei around the neck. Excellent condition.
Comments: Common and available.
Courtesy of: Angie's Doll Boutique
Price Range: $120.00-175.00

Name: "No Name" Female - Baby (Topsy-type)
Maker's Name: Unmarked
Marks: None
Origin: U.S.A.
Size: 11″
Date: circa 1920s-1940s
Description: All composition baby body with molded hair deeply curled and tinted with 3 tufts of human hair, painted features, fully jointed with all original clothing. Excellent condition.
Comments: Available and plentiful.
Courtesy of: Angie's Doll Boutique
Price Range: $90.00-125.00

Name: "No Name" Female - Baby
Maker's Name: Unmarked
Marks: None
Origin: U.S.A.
Size: 6½″
Date: circa 1920s-1940s
Description: All composition baby body with painted features, molded deep curled hair with human hair tufts, original clothing, fully jointed chubby body. Excellent condition.
Comments: Unusually small example of a common style doll. Scarce size.
Courtesy of: Angie's Doll Boutique
Price Range: $75.00-95.00

Name: Christening Baby
Maker's Name: Unmarked
Marks: None
Origin: U.S.A.
Size: 6¾"
Date: 1920s-1940s
Description: Brown all-composition baby body with original clothing. Molded tinted hair. Fully jointed. Excellent condition.
Comments: Common style of doll with an uncommon outfit.
Courtesy of: Angie's Doll Boutique
Price Range: $75.00-95.00

Name: "No Name" Female - Girl
Maker's Name: Unmarked
Marks: None
Origin: U.S.A.
Size: 14½"
Date: circa 1930s-1940s
Description: Brown composition head with painted molded features on a child's stuffed cloth brown body, jointed, wool hair, original clothing and shoes. Doll has "snaps" in her stitched palms (hands). The arms are believed to have held a smaller doll or object. Excellent condition.
Comments: Available
Courtesy of: Angie's Doll Boutique
Price Range: $65.00-95.00

Name: Dancing Couple
Maker's Name: New Orleans (no company name)
Marks: New Orleans (paper label)
Origin: U.S.A.
Size: 5¼" each
Date: circa 1930s-1950s
Description: Tourist dolls made of papier-mache heads, molded painted features with cloth wrapped wire bodies. Female has wool wig and male has molded tinted hair. Both dolls have original dancing outfits made of cotton and satin-lacy sleeves. Exaggerated features. Good condition.
Comments: Plentiful.
Courtesy of: Angie's Doll Boutique
Price Range: $75.00-100.00 pair

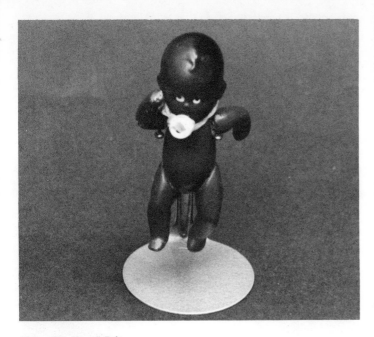

Name: "No Name" Baby
Maker's Name: Unmarked
Marks: None
Origin: U.S.A.
Size: 2¾"
Date: circa 1920s-1940s
Description: Miniature brown chubby body baby with composition molded painted features, open mouth with an original pacifier held in the mouth by a ribbon. Fully jointed. Excellent condition.
Comments: Scarce, doll in a unique size. Finely detailed features.
Courtesy of: Angie's Doll Boutique
Price Range: $65.00-90.00

Name: "No Name" Female - Baby
Maker's Name: Armand Marseille
Marks: Armand Marseille Germany
Origin: Germany
Size: 19½"
Date: circa 1910-1930
Description: Brown composition head with molded tinted hair, brown glass inset eyes, open mouth with 2 teeth, composition 5-piece body. (Redressed). Excellent condition.
Comments: Well made. Available.
Courtesy of: Yesteryear's Museum
Price Range: $375.00-600.00

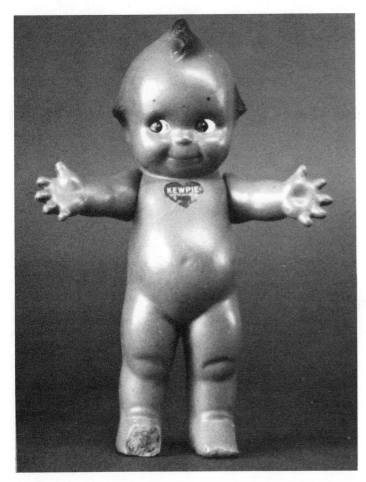

Name: Hottentot (Black Kewpie)
Maker's Name: Rose O'Neill
Marks: (Heart Shape) Kewpie by Rose O'Neill (inside the heart)
Origin: U.S.A.
Size: 11"
Date: circa 1913
Description: Brown all-composition male doll with jointed arms, red heart-shaped decal on the upper chest, molded tinted curly-top hair, black dots for brows, side glancing eyes, tiny red painted wings on the upper back. Good condition. *Damage to right foot.
Comments: Signed Kewpie(s) in Black versions are scarce.
Price Range: $200.00-275.00

Name: Maggie Head Kane Doll
Maker's Name: Maggie Head Kane
Marks: None
Origin: U.S.A.
Size: 22"
Date: circa 1950s
Description: Elderly brown composition doll with wooden hands, cloth body. The shoulder-head exhibits strong Negroid features rendered in a naturalistic manner, deeply molded painted hair, greenish brown eyes, brass earrings, raised molded painted eye brows. Doll has sewn jointed knees. All original clothing. Excellent condition.
Comments: Fine example of a mid 20th century artist doll.
Price Range: $220.00-285.00

Name: Patsy
Maker's Name: Effanbee
Marks: EFFANBEE
Origin: U.S.A.
Size: 17"
Date: circa 1920s-1940s
Description: All composition warm brown girl's body with molded painted features and hair. Blue sleep eyes, swivel head, molded hair and painted red lips. Excellent condition. (Redressed).
Comments: Black Patsy dolls are available but not plentiful.
Price Range: $325.00-380.00

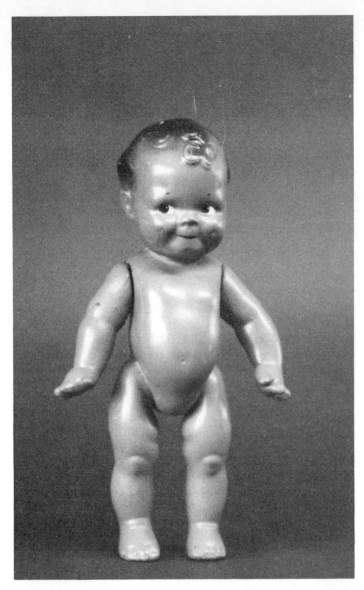

Name: Scootles
Maker's Name: Rose O'Neill
Marks: None
Origin: U.S.A.
Size: 12″
Date: circa 1925
Description: Impish smiling brown composition male with a chubby toddler baby, molded deep curled hair tinted black/brown, fully jointed, painted molded features, dots used for eyebrows. Excellent condition.
Comments: Available but not plentiful.
Price Range: $400.00-500.00

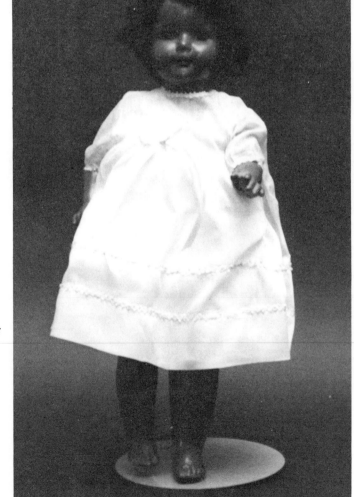

Name: Rosemary
Maker's Name: Effanbee
Marks: EFFANBEE "Rosemary" Walk-Talk-Sleep (printed inside of an oval)
Origin: U.S.A.
Size: 17¼″
Date: circa 1920s-1930s
Description: Brown composition head, arms and legs with glassine sleep eyes, mohair wig, cloth body, open mouth, 4 teeth. Excellent condition.
Comments: Character doll, non-ethnic features. Available but not plentiful.
Courtesy of: Yesteryear's Museum
Price Range: $220.00-300.00

Name: Aunt Jemima
Maker's Name: Unmarked
Marks: None
Origin: U.S.A.
Size: 7″
Date: circa 1920s
Description: Papier-mache female adult with exaggerated painted features, open mouth with white painted teeth, cloth body. Doll holds a lid from a cooking pot in her left hand. Doll is believed to be a dollhouse figure. Original clothing. Excellent condition.
Comments: Common style and available.
Courtesy of: Yesteryear's Museum
Price Range: $90.00-140.00

Name: "No Name" Female - Girl
Maker's Name: Société Francaise de Fabrication de Bébés & Jouets
Marks: S.F.B.J.
Origin: France
Size: 8¼″
Date: circa 1920s
Description: Brown composition doll, jointed child's body in a soft warm brown tone, glass inset brown eyes, closed mouth with a mohair wig. Original clothing. Good condition.
Comments: "Late" example of the dolls produced by S.F.B.J.
Courtesy of: Yesteryear's Museum
Price Range: $275.00-325.00

Name: Norah Wellings
Maker's Name: Attributed to Norah Wellings
Marks: None
Origin: England
Size: 7″
Date: circa 1926-1960
Description: Brown felt female child's body with a composition mask face, molded painted features, open/closed mouth with painted teeth, mohair wig, strong Negroid features. Original grass skirt with opposite bangles on feet and arms. Excellent condition.
Comments: More readily available than a signed Norah Wellings creation.
Courtesy of: Yesteryear's Museum
Price Range: $140.00-200.00

Name: Milliner's Model
Maker's Name: Unmarked
Marks: None
Origin: U.S.A.
Size: 6″
Date: circa 1860-1890s
Description: All original finely executed papier-mache female adult doll, representing a model. Molded painted Negroid features, painted mache head & hands, wooden legs with painted green boots, well made leather body, molded hair in a curly 19th century style. Original clothing, carrying a tiny handmade basket believed to have been made on a Georgia Island. The hat is woven with flowers and ribbon attached (original). Excellent condition.

Comments: Milliner's Model is a term coined during the mid 19th century. It refers to well made papier-mache dolls with leather bodies. The word "milliner" refers to a person who makes women hats.
Courtesy of: Charlene Upham Collection
Price Range: $625.00-775.00

Name: "No Name" Male - Boy
Maker's Name: Unmarked
Marks: None
Origin: Germany
Size: 12″
Date: circa 1890s-1920s
Description: Black painted composition doll with composition arms, hands and legs, with a cloth body. Doll has raised molded brows, inset brown glass eyes, open mouth with 4 lower teeth and 2 upper teeth. Dressed in short pants, shirt, sweater and original sweater cap. Bare feet. Doll has a smiling face. Excellent condition. Rough composition texture.
Comments: Available but not plentiful. Male dolls from the late 19th and early 20th centuries are highly sought after.
Courtesy of: Heidepriem Collection
Price Range: $200.00-275.00

Name: "No Name" Male - Boy
Maker's Name: Unmarked
Marks: None
Origin: Germany
Size: 18"
Date: circa 1880-1920s
Description: Papier-mache head with stationary brown glass eyes, painted red lips, open mouth with 4 teeth, wooden body and limbs, feet have painted shoes. Brass cymbals in each hand. Doll is painted a dark brown, wearing original clothing. Mouth is hinged at the lower lip, original human hair wig, double sided hat (red night cap inside top-hat).
Comments: Scarce
Courtesy of: Yesteryear's Museum
Price Range: $300.00-400.00

Name: No-Name
Maker's Name: Unmarked
Marks: None
Origin: Germany
Size: 10¾"
Date: circa 1880-1900
Description: Male doll dressed as a musical performer. Squeeze the tummy and doll sticks out his tongue and claps the cymbals. Doll has a papier mache head, wooden arms and legs, painted white eyes with black pupils. Excellent condition.
Comments: Common.
Courtesy of: Ron Carr Collection
Price Range: $500.00-600.00

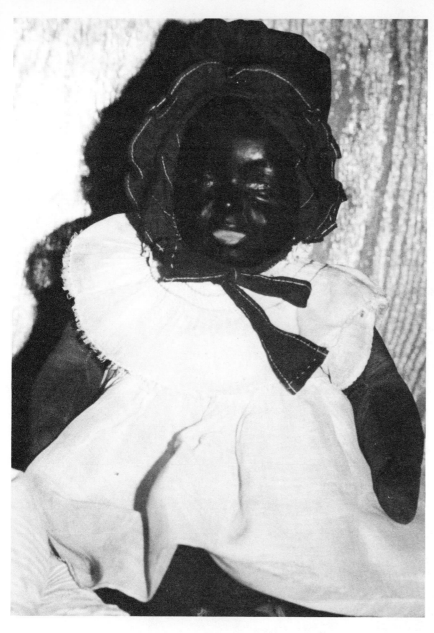

Name: Kaiser Baby-type
Maker's Name: Attributed to Kaiser Doll Co.
Marks: None
Origin: Germany
Size: 11½″
Date: circa 1900-1920s
Description: Dark brown composition head of a female baby on a plush warm brown body, well constructed, inset brown glass eyes, molded detailed nose with an open/closed mouth. Strong naturalistic Negroid features. Excellent condition.
Comments: Composition Black dolls made with such care and detail are scarce and eagerly sought after.
Courtesy of: Fairhaven Doll Museum
Price Range: $180.00-225.00

Name: No-Name
Maker's Name: Unmarked
Marks: None
Origin: Germany
Size: 5¼″
Date: circa 1880-1900
Description: All papier mache doll with molded painted features, jointed arms and legs, mohair wig. Originally nude. Excellent condition.
Comments: Common.
Courtesy of: Ron Carr Collection
Price Range: $100.00-175.00

Name: No-Name
Maker's Name: Unmarked
Marks: None
Origin: Germany
Size: 13" each
Date: circa 1880-1890s

Comments: Scarce.
Courtesy of: Ron Carr Collection
Price Range: $850.00-950.00 pair

Description: Papier mache shoulder plate dolls with mache arms and legs. Bodies stuffed cloth, painted boots, paper hat on the male, papier mache hat on the female. Glass inset eyes, painted molded features. Press tummy and the dolls squeak. Redressed. Excellent condition.

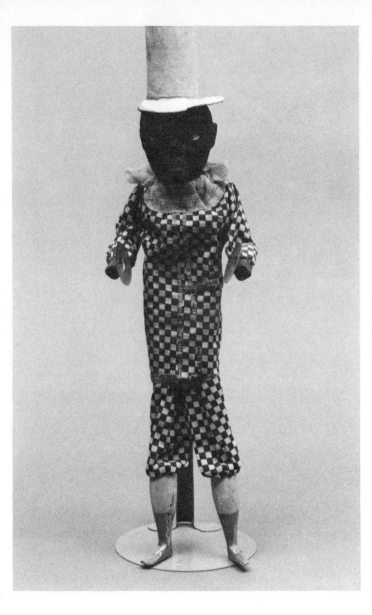

Name: No-Name
Maker's Name: Unmarked
Marks: None
Origin: Germany
Size: 17″
Date: circa 1880-1915
Description: Papier mache head, wooden arms, legs and torso. Molded painted features. Cymbals attached to the doll's hands. Original clothing. Top hat squeaks when pressed down. Excellent condition.
Comments: Scarce.
Courtesy of: Ron Carr Collection
Price Range: $650.00-900.00

Name: Topsy Turvy
Maker's Name: Unmarked
Marks: None
Origin: Germany
Size: 8¼″
Date: circa 1880-1900s
Description: Papier mache "Topsy Turvy" doll with composition arms. Black doll with brown glass inset eyes, black human hair. White doll has blue inset eyes and blonde hair. Jointed arms, cloth stuffed bodies. Excellent condition.
Comments: Common.
Courtesy of: V. Mackemull Collection
Price Range: $195.00-300.00

179

Name: Topsy Turvy
Maker's Name: Unmarked
Marks: None
Origin: Germany
Size: 9″
Date: circa 1880-1900
Description: Papier-mache heads on both ends of the cloth body. Black doll has mohair wig. White doll has blonde mohair wig, glass stationary eyes, ethnic features, arms on both dolls are made of papier-mache, painted red lips. Excellent condition.
Comments: Scarce but not available.
Courtesy of: Yesteryear's Museum
Price Range: $300.00-375.00

Name: No-Name
Maker's Name: Unmarked
Marks: None
Origin: U.S.A.
Size: 9½″ (doll), 7½″ (carriage)
Date: circa 1900-1930s
Description: Brown painted composition doll, fully jointed with wide flat-shaped legs (hinged at the hips). Doll has painted features, naturalistic rendering and the doll is pushing a composition carriage with metal wheels. Both are in excellent condition.
Comments: Scarce.
Courtesy of: Ron Carr Collection
Price Range: $275.00-335.00

Terminology

Adtocolite - Lightweight material similar to composition in appearance, used during the early 1900's. When this material cracks it makes circular bands.

Alabama Babies - Dolls made in Roanoke, Alabama c. 1904-24 by Mrs. Ella Smith, Alabama Indestructible Doll.

All - Original - Doll, doll parts, clothing and accessories remain intact. Doll may or may not be played with.

Americana - Both a term and a description of items made in America (USA) and an overall link to American history.

Apple-head doll - Dolls with heads made of dried shrunken apples inspired by American Indian doll-makers. Once the apple is shrunken, the wrinkles add character lines to the face.

Applied ears - Ears are added to the head, not a part of the original mold or design.

Armature - Doll's frame made of wire or wood and covered by a top material.

Articulated - Well-defined, usually referring to fingers, limbs or toes.

Attributed to - Artist given credit without any marks being present.

Aunt Jemima - A term used to describe dolls with matronly characteristics. The original Aunt Jemima dolls were made of paper - circa 1905 by the R.T. Davis Company, then in cloth. The R.T. Davis Company changed its name to Aunt Jemima Mills in 1914 and was later acquired by the Quaker Oats Company - circa 1926. It is believed that Aunt Jemima was represented in person by Nancy Green of Missouri.

Automation - Mechanical device that allows a doll human-like movement. Often times a clockwork mechanism is used.

Baby doll - Doll representing an infant usually with chubby features.

Ball jointed - A ball used to separate and allow full movement of joints.

Bebe - Doll representing a baby during the late 19th century by French and German manufacturers.

Bent limb baby - 20th century technique used for baby and toddler babies which allows easy sitting position of the dolls.

Bisque - 19th century hard material used to fashion doll heads and limbs. This material has a matte finish and often times is tinted in the slip to create well made Black dolls. Others may be painted black or brown after modeling is completed.

Bottle doll - Early 19th to mid 20th century dolls fashioned to resemble Black servants. The dolls were used as playthings and doorstops. The bottles were filled with sand, top portion of the dolls made of cloth wearing long dresses. Origin USA, South and North Eastern regions.

Broom doll - Late 19th - mid 20th century dolls of cloth made around a broom handle for decorative purposes. Some of the dolls were elaborately dressed. Origin USA.

Can't break 'em - A hard substance used to fashion composition dolls created by the Horsman Doll Company and other USA companies during the early 20th century. The can't break 'em material was break resistant.

Caricature features - Features exaggerated to merely resemble the person portrayed.

Carved features - Features carved by hand or a tool, usually painted to accent certain characteristics.

Celebrity doll - Dolls that were made to honor and portray famous figures, i.e., Louis Armstrong doll, Shirley Temple, etc.

Celluloid - A very thin material that is brittle and resembles bisque when tinted before hardening. Cheaply made dolls are painted after the dolls have been modeled. Early Black celluloid dolls are rare. (Resembles thin plastic).

Change-O-head - Dolls made during the late 19th century with changeable heads which often included at least one Black head. These heads were made of bisque and composition.

Character doll - 20th century development of dolls with realistic humanoid features.

China - Glazed porcelain that contains Kaolin to produce a hard glass-like finish. Black china dolls are scarce.

Circa - A term used to date decorative items which allows 20 years on either side; round-about.

Claw-shaped - A term used to describe the claw shape of hands on cloth dolls. The thumb is separate and the other fingers are molded as one.

Closed mouth - Lips are pressed together.

Composition - A fiber, wood and glue compound used to fashion dolls during the late 19th to mid 20th century. Black dolls may have brown or black coloring added to the mixture, or may be painted after the baking process.

Cottage industry - Small industries usually operated in the home by an individual or family member i.e., Izannah Walker, one of the first USA dollmakers. Black Izannah Walker dolls are scarce.

Coo voice - Voice box that mimicks the sound of a baby at play. Many early 20th century dolls have coo voice boxes.

Cork - The same type of cork used to plug glass bottles was also used to stuff the bodies of dolls during the early 20th century.

Cornhusk doll - Dolls made of cornhusk clothing usually with a buckeye or nut head. Dolls made of tobacco leaves were also fashioned by similar techniques. Black cornhusk dolls are scarce. Currently being reproduced.

Craft doll - Usually created as a decorative item rather than a plaything. These dolls are created by crafts artisans in guilds or home (cottage) productions.

Crazing - Usually refers to the cracking which occurs with composition dolls exposed to adverse temperatures.

Crown - Top of the head often times left open in bisque dolls. A piece of cardboard or plaster is used to cover the opening.

Cry box - A box found in late 19th - mid 20th century dolls mimicking the crying sound of a baby.

Curled hair - Straight hair in a curled style.

Curly hair - Each strand of hair is curled tightly.

Depose' - French word for company registry, abbreviated Dep. The German dollmakers abbreviation is the same for their trademark word **deponiert**. Depose' or Dep. is often included in a doll's markings.

Dome head - Bisque round head, solid dome, not halved.

Doll artist - Dollmaker, not mass produced by machinery. Doll artist is also a term used to describe mass produced dolls designed by doll artists for large companies, "Doll artist dolls" i.e., Polly and Pete circa 1950's by Horsman Doll Inc. Polly and Pete are Black dolls (twins) and have striking negroid features.

Dynel hair - A very thin synthetic hair that may be used for wigs or rooted in the doll's head. This type of hair was popular during the mid 1950's.

Embossed - Raised lettering usually found on the nape of the doll's neck bearing the name and maker's mark. Can also be found on the doll's bottom.

Exaggerated features - Black dolls exhibiting large eyes, mouth or noses overexaggerated to appear comical or make a statement.

Excellent condition - Refers to a doll removed from its original box but in unaltered condition.

Fairy skin - A soft vinyl skin developed by the Horsman Doll Company. The skin is pliable and flesh-like to the touch and tinted a mellow brown color. Also pink flesh-tone for white dolls.

Fashion doll - Well-dressed female dolls wearing fashions of their times or dressed to reflect an earlier time period. Black fashion dolls are rare.

Fired - A technique used to dry bisque dolls and apply glaze to china dolls.

Five-piece body - Head, arms and legs are jointed creating a fully jointed 5-piece body.

Flange Neck/legs - A doll's head or legs attached to a cloth body by a wire or plastic clamp wrapped around the groove of the body part and embedded in the cloth. Flanged limbs have very little mobility.

Fleeced hair - Wool hair dyed the appropriate color cut short and curled. Fleeced hair was used for Black dolls made during the late 18th century to present. The naturally curly texture of the wool proved suitable to represent American and foreign Black races' hair.

Flirting eyes - Eyes that move from side to side.

Flocked hair - Sheared wool sparsely placed on a boy's or baby doll's head to represent hair fuzz.

Floss - Loosely twisted silk or cotton embroidery thread used for hair tufts in topknot dolls' heads or wigs.

Folk art - Objects created by hand or hand tools. Simplicity and boldness are characteristic of such items. Utilitarian items such as clothes pins, potato mashers and brooms are used to create dolls.

Fork hands - Stick-like hands usually found on Peg-wooden dolls to articulate fingers.

Full lips/mouth - Fleshy large lips usually found on Black dolls with negroid features.

Fully jointed - Doll that has jointed neck, arms and legs.

Glass eyes - Porcelain or blown glass eyes with or without pupils. Varies in colors.

Glassine eyes - Simulated glass eyes, plastic substance used since the mid 20th century.

Glazed - A technique used to apply a glass-like finish to bisque or pottery. China dolls are glazed and bisque is unglazed. Black china dolls made prior to the 20th century are rare.

Golliwog - A doll created from a character in a 19th century English children's fairy tale. African-Black features exaggerated.

Good condition - A doll without a box, played with or handled and remains intact with little to no replaced parts.

Googly eyes - Glass or tinted large cartoon-like eyes often times side glancing.

Gutta-percha - A 19th century substance made of a latex compound to fashion dolls. Black gutta-percha dolls are extremely rare.

Half doll - Top portion of a doll with a bottom usually fashioned into a utilitarian bottom, i.e., pincushion, weighted container (doorstop) etc. Black dolls usually have cloth top-halves. White dolls may be found in china or bisque.

Hatted doll - Ceramic dolls with a molded hat attached to their heads, made during the late 19th to early 20th century. Black hatted dolls are scarce.

Head-kerchief - A head scarf found on matronly-type Black female dolls.

Impish - Doll with a slight smile, raised eye brows, eyes to the side and curled lip (mischievous look).

Jointed - Movable limbs on dolls.

Jumper-doll - A black or white doll with moveable joints that display dance-like movements when a stick is placed into a hole in their backs. These dolls are usually made entirely of wood with flat bodies and stick-like rounded limbs. They may be referred to as "Dancers" or "Stick dolls".

Kapok - Padding used to stuff dolls, made from the fiber of a tree pod. A silky cotton fiber.

Kerchief - A term used to describe the bandana type of triangular folded cloth around the necks and shoulders of Black male and female dolls. They may be also found on some white folk art dolls.

Kid body - Young goat skin covering used to make all or part of a doll's body that is stained with dyes to produce a brown or black color for Black dolls. Kid body dolls have been made since the 17th century.

Knitted doll - A doll made entirely of a knitted fabric, popular during the early 20th century. Many Black knitted dolls were made for decorations and as a plaything.

Lathe-turned - A doll turned on lathe and chiseled as it is turned to create a shape. Wooden dolls are molded by this technique. Wooden Black dolls are scarce.

Lithographed - An image printed on cloth, either a lithographed face or the entire body, e.g., Aunt Jemima-Uncle Moses Family.

Low-brow - A term used to describe a doll wearing a hairstyle that is close to the eyebrows. Low-brow hairstyles are common on bisque dolls.

MIB - A term and abbreviation used to describe a doll that is untouched and still in its original box, **Mint** and **In the Box**.

Mama-voice - A voice box that repeats the word "mama", found in dolls popular during the early 20th century. The voice box is activated when the doll is handled.

Mammy doll - A description of a Black matronly female doll which portrayed a maid servant.

Manikin doll - A doll used for display only. Manikin dolls are usually made of a plaster compound or rigid plastic. Black manikin dolls made of early plaster are uncommon but available, rigid plastic ones are more common. Occasionally found in wood.

Marked/Marks - Any numbers or names found on dolls made from molds. Many early Black dolls do not have visible marks to help identify their makers.

Mask-face - The face of a doll applied to a half-head usually found on cloth dolls and made of a glue and cloth compound to make modeling of features more detailed. The half-head is split vertically from the crown (top) to the chin.

Mechanical doll - A doll that has movement activated by a mechanism similar to a clock's works. Black mechanical dolls are highly prized and scarce from the 19th and early 20th centuries. Particularly, French made versions.

Mint condition - A doll that is unplayed with and all-original.

Mitten hands - Hands shaped like mittens with the thumb separate and the other four fingers rounded into one smooth shape. Some mitten-hands may have stitches in them to simulate fingers.

Modeling - A term used to describe an accurate shaping or forming of a doll or doll part.

Mohair wig - Angora goat hair used for wigs.

Mold - An apparatus used to pour or press the heads of dolls. Molds may also have numbers embossed into them which is transferred to the dolls' head, i.e., "mold number".

Mold number - See "mold".

Molded features - The features of a doll created by a mold rather than being fashioned by hand or a tool.

Mortise-and-tenon - A joint used mainly in wooden dolls that allows full range of movement. The joint is hinged in a socket. Black dolls with the above joints are considered extremely well-made and scarce.

Multi-face doll - A doll with multiple faces on a single head that can be changed by rotating it or changing a removable mask.

Naturalistic features - Features that are not altered or exaggerated from the intended portrayed image. Early Black dolls with naturalistic features are scarce.

Negroid features - A Black doll with specially designed features to capture the character and true likeness of a Black person. Few early Black dolls had both naturalistic and negroid features. Often times a Black doll was made from the same mold as a white doll and then painted brown or black.

Nipple doll - Dolls made from baby bottle nipples, left intact and dressed in matronly clothing to represent an older Black lady. The doll has painted features and may have hair or a head-kerchief.

Nut-head doll - A doll with a head made of a variety of nuts, i.e., pecans, walnuts, hazelnuts and buckeyes. The bodies of these dolls may be found in cloth or straw.

Oil painted features - Doll's features painted with oil paint.

Open-closed mouth - The doll's lips are parted but there isn't an actual opening in the head.

Open-mouth with hole - The doll's lips are parted and a round hole is in the middle for a nursing bottle. Nursing holes began appearing in dolls made during the mid 20th century to present.

Painted eyes - Eyes that have been affixed by paint. Painted eyes may appear on dolls made in all mediums.

Paperweight eyes - Eyes that have a weighted mechanism which enables them to open and close.

Papier-mache - A paper pulp mixture with glue to form a harden substance. Papier mache is easily molded but is very brittle and fragile. Few 18th and 19th century papier mache dolls have survived. Black papier mache dolls from the above centuries are rare.

Pate - Top of a doll's head. The cut-away portion of the head that is bald and usually covered by a wig.

Patent - Any invention or technique that is registered with a national patent office. Patented items are issued identification numbers.

Patent date - A series of numbers that include the date of patent registration. Patent dates are useful only to determine the registration date. An item/doll may carry the patent date for an indefinite time period.

Patina - A mellowed and warm finish that is acquired with age on the surface of Black bisque and wooden dolls.

Peddler doll - A doll that is representative of a vendor, usually carrying small trays. Early vendor dolls were popular during the 19th century in England and the 20th century in America. Black vendor dolls can be found in a variety of materials such as wax, cloth with wire frames and wood.

Peg-wooden doll - All-wooden dolls with carved and lathe turned body parts. Fully jointed. In the USA, New England was the area of production for Peg-woodens during the late 19th and early 20th centuries.

Personality doll - See "Celebrity Doll".

Piccaninny - Also spelled Pickaninny. Refers to a small Black child. The child may have numerous braids in his or her hair.

Portrait doll - Doll with recognizable features of prominent individuals.

Poured-wax doll - Doll made by pouring wax into a mold rather than molding it by hand.

Pouty - Character doll of a small child with lips protruding or with dismayed expression.

Premium - Of the finest quality or a term used to describe the high demand of a doll. Black dolls are referred to as being highly collectible or of a **premium** in today's market.

Pull strings - Strings on the outside of a doll's body that operate automated movement.

Rag dolls - All cloth dolls.

Saran hair - Hair made from a vinyl compound during the mid 20th century in the USA.

Sculptured features - Chiseled, well defined features.

Sew holes - Holes found in the breast portion of a shoulder plate in which strings are sewn into the body for attachment.

S.G.D.G. - Abbreviation for the French word "sans garantie du gouvernement", meaning that no patent has been researched and thus does not have government protection of a manufacturer's patent. French dolls may bear the above initials.

Slip - A liquid clay and water mixture cast in a mold. Some Black dolls may have brown slips to give the needed color to their complexion. Slips are also used to mend or bind ceramic pieces and to apply decoration.

Slit-head - A cut in a wax doll's head made to insert hair. The crown of the doll's head is cut in a circular pattern and the hair is placed under the wax.

Socket head - A swivel head that fits into a shoulder plate or body.

Spoon hand - A crude hand usually made of wood that lacks articulated fingers but may have a thumb. Spoon hands are cup-shaped.

Spring-jointed - Joints that are operated by metal springs.

Stockinet - Cotton-stocking fabric popular during the 19th and 20th centuries.

Stringing - A technique used to attach limbs to a doll's body by elastic cord.

Toddler body - Body of a young child with stubby or chubby features.

Trademark - An identifying symbol or name used by a manufacturer.

Tuck comb - Elongated wooden comb carved and decorated, found on peg-wood dolls' coiffures.

Utility doll - A doll with a body fashioned from a common household object such as a potato masher, broom, shaving brush, bell or bottle.

Wiry hair (kinky or nappy) - Hair style used for Black dolls. Straight short crinkly hair.

Bibliography of Books on Dolls

A Book of Dolls & Doll Houses. Flora, Gill. C.E. Tuttle Co., Rutland, VT, 1967.

Collector Books. Paducah, KY.

A Detailed Listing and Value Guide to Barbie Doll Fashions. Amundsen, Joan. Plainview, NY.

A Fabulous Dollhouse of the Twenties. Noble, John. Dover Publications, New York, 1976.

A Portfolio of Armand Marseille Dolls. Guthrie, Dorothy L. D.L. Guthrie, 1981.

A Treasury of Beautiful Dolls. Noble, John. New York. Hawthorne Book, 1971.

Advertising Dolls. Robison, Joleen A. Collector Books. Paducah, KY, 1980.

Alexander's Rag Line. Hunter, Marsha Trentham. C.R. Hunter Print Co. Knoxville, TN, 1982.

American Folk Dolls. Lavitt, Wendy. Knopf. New York, 1982.

An Illustrated Price Guide to Collectible Barbie Dolls. Manos, Susan & Paris. Collector Books. Paducah, KY, 1982.

Armand Marseille Dolls. Smith, Patricia R. Collector Books. Paducah, KY, 1981.

Artists and Original Dolls. Ross, Joan M. J.M. Ross. New York, NY, 1983.

The Beloved Kathe-Kruse Dolls. Richter, Lydia. Hobby House Press. Cumberland, MD, 1983.

A Century of Celluloid Dolls. Buchholz, Shirley. Hobby House Press. Cumberland, MD, 1983.

Charakterpuppen. Richter, Lydia. Laterna Magica. Munchen, 1983.

Collectible Barbie Dolls. DeWein, Sibyl St. John. DeWein, 1980.

Collectible Dolls in National Costume. Axe, John. Hobby House Press. Riverdale, MD, 1977.

The Collector's Encyclopedia of Dolls. Coleman, Dorothy S. Crown Publishers, New York, 1968.

Collecting Figural Doorstops. Hamburger, Marilyn G. A.S. Barnes. South Brunswick, NJ, 1978.

Collecting German Dolls. Bach, Jean. L. Stewart. Secaucus, NJ, 1983.

The Collector's Guide to British Dolls Since 1920. Mansell, Colette. R. Hale. London, 1983.

The Collector's History of Dolls. King, Constance Eileen. St. Martin's Press. New York, 1977/78.

The Collector's History of Dolls. King, Constance Eileen. Bonanza Books. New York, 1977, 1981.

Delightful Dolls, Antique and Otherwise. Bateman, Thelma. Hobby House Press. Washington, 1966.

Dolls. Fawcett, Clara Evelyn. C.T. Branford Co. Boston, 1964.

Dolls and Doll-makers. Hillier, Mary. Putnam. New York, 1968.

The Dolls' House. Wilckens, Leonie von. Bell & Hyman. London, 1980.

Dolls. Noble, John. Walker. New York, 1967.

Dolls' Houses in America. Jacobs, Flora Gill. Scribner. New York, 1974.

Dolls in Color. Darrah, Marjorie Merritt. Wallace-Homestead Book Co. Des Moines, IA, 1971.

Dolls: Makers and Marks. Coleman, Elizabeth A. Washington, 1966.

Dolls the Wide World Over. Bachmann, Manfred. Crown Publishers. New York, 1973.

Dorothey Heizer, the Artist and her Dolls. Krechniak, Helen Bullard. National Institute of American Doll Artists. New York, 1972.

Effanbee. Axe, John. Hobby House Press. Cumberland, MD, 1983.

Effanbee Dolls. Schoonmaker, Patricia N. Hobby House Press. Cumberland, MD, 1984.

Effanbee, Dolls That Touch Your Heart. Smith, Patricia R. Collector Books. Paducah, KY, 1983.

The Encyclopedia of Celebrity Dolls. Axe, John. Hobby House Press. Cumberland, MD, 1983.

English Dolls' Houses of the Eighteenth and Nineteenth Centuries. Green, Vivien. Scribner. New York, 1979.

European and American Dolls and Their Marks and Patents. White, Gwen. Putnam. New York, 1966.

European and American Dolls. White, Gwen. Crescent Books. New York, 1982.

Family Dolls' Houses. Greene, Vivien. C.T. Brandford Co. Newton, MA, 1973.

Family Dolls' Houses. Greene, Vivien. Bell. London, 1973.

Focusing on Effanbee Composition Dolls. Foulke, Jan. Hobby House Press. Riverdale, MD, 1978.

Folk and Foreign Costume Dolls. Frame, Linda. Collector Books. Paducah, KY, 1980.

Four Dolls' Houses--Plus Two. Hosmer, Herbert Henry. Toy Cupboard Museums. Lancaster, MA, 1973.

French Dolls. Smith, Patricia R. Collector Books. Paducah, KY, 1981.

German Dolls. Smith, Patricia R. Collector Books. Paducah, KY.

Grandmother's Adobe Dollhouse. Smith, MaryLou M. New Mexico Magazine. Santa Fe, NM, 1984.

Handbook of Collectible Dolls. Merrill, Madelaine O. Melrose, MA, 1969.

Heubach's Little Characters. Stanton, Carol. Living Dolls. Enfield England, 1978.

Japanese Antique Dolls. Gribbin, Will. Weatherhill, New York, 1984.

The Jumeau Doll. Whitton, Margaret. Dover, New York, 1980.

Kathe Kruse Puppen. Richter, Lydia. Laterna Magica. Munchen, 1983.

Kestner, King of Dollmakers. Foulke, Jan. Hobby House Press. Cumberland, MD, 1982.

Kestner and Simon & Halbig Dolls. Smith, Patricia R. Collector Books. Paducah, KY, 1976.

Lewis Sorensen's Doll Scrapbook. Sorensen, Lewis. Thor Publications, Alhambra, CA, 1976.

Madame Alexander's American Beauties. Theriault, Florence. Gold Horse Pub. Annapolis, MD, 1983.

Madame Alexander Catalog Reprints. McKeon, B.J. Brockton, MA, 1984.

Madame Alexander Collector's Dolls. Smith, Patricia R. Collector Books. Paducah, KY, 1978.

Madame Alexander Collector's Dolls II. Smith, Patricia R. Collector Books. Paducah, KY, 1981.

Madame Alexander Dolls Are Made With Love. Uhl, Marjorie V. Sturges. M.V.S. Uhl. Mapleton, IA, 1983.

Madame Alexander Dolls on Review. Uhl, Marjorie V. Sturges. Taylor Publishing Co. Dallas, TX, 1981.

Madame Alexander "Little People". Biggs, Marge. Biggs. Riverside, CA, 1979.

More American Beauties. Theriault, Florence. Gold Horse Pub. Annapolis, MD, 1984.

"The Most Beautiful Dolls . . ." Are Made by Madame Alexander. Thomas, Jane Ruggles. Comox Books. San Diego, CA, 1977.

Nancy Ann Storybook Dolls. Miller, Marjorie A. Hobby House Press. Cumberland, MD, 1980.

Orientalem. Richter, Lydia. Laterna Magica. Munchen, 1982.

Paper Dolls, How to Find, Recognize, Buy, Collect and Sell the Cutouts of Two Centuries. Wallach, Anne Tolstoi. Van Nostrand Reinhold. New York, 1982.

Paper Dolls and Their Artists. Young, Mary. Young. Kettering, OH.

Pollock's History of English Dolls & Toys. Fawdry, Kenneth. Benn. London, 1979.

Pollock's Dictionary of English Dolls. Crown. New York, 1983.

Price Guide to the Twentieth Century Dolls Series. Glassmire, Carol Gast. Wallace-Homestead Book Co. Des Moines, IA, 1981.

Price Guide to the Twentieth Century Dolls Series. Glassmire, Carol Gast. Wallace-Homestead Book Co. Des Moines, IA, 1983.

Queen Mary's Dolls' House and Dolls Belonging to H.M. the Queen. Musgrave, Clifford. Pitkin Pictorials. London, 1967.

Rhoda Shoemaker's Price Guide for Madame Alexander Dolls. Shoemaker, Rhoda. Shoemaker. Menlo Park, CA, 1977.

The Royalty of Paper Dolls. Krebs, Marta K. Hobby House Press. Cumberland, MD, 1984.

Schoenhut Dolls & Toys. Manos, Susan. Collector Books. Paducah, KY, 1976.

M. Elaine and Dan Buser's Guide to Schoenhut's Dolls, Toys and Circus, 1872-1976. Busera, M. Elaine. Collector Books. Paducah, KY, 1976.

Simon & Halbig Dolls. Foulke, Jan. Hobby House. Cumberland. MD, 1984.

Terri Lee, From the 40s to the 60s. Hencey, Naomi. November House. Battle Creek, MI, 1984.

Toys and Dolls Made in Occupied Japan. Chandler, Ceil. Chandler's Discriminating Junk. Houston, TX, 1973.

Treasury of Kathe Kruse Dolls. Richter, Ludia. HP Books. Tucson, AZ, 1984.

Treasury of Mme. Alexander Dolls. Foulke, Jan. Hobby House Press. Riverdale, MD, 1979.

Victorian Dolls' Houses and Their Furnishings. Jacobs, Flora Gill. Washington Dolls' House & Toy Museum. Washington, 1978.

The Warner Collectors' Guide to Dolls. Bach, Jean. Warner Books. New York, 1982.

Wee Friends. Watson, Eleanor Schwingle. Watson. Little Rock, AR, 1974.

Wonderful Dolls of Papier Mache. Gerken, Jo Elizabeth. Doll Research Associates. Lincoln, NE, 1970.

The World of Barbie Dolls. Manos, Susan and Paris. Collector Books. Paducah, KY, 1983.

Books With Black Dolls Listed (Not Price Guides)

A Century of Celluloid Dolls, Buchholz, Shirley, 1983 Hobby House Press, Cumberland, MD
1. "No-Name", Celluloid; p. 28,d ark brown; painted hair, molded brown painted eyes and upper eyelashes; open mouth tongue painted red; marked with a turtle in a diamond shaped design. Non-ethnic jointed.
2. "Mo-Name", Celluloid; p. 32, Maurine Popp Collection. Jointed; molded black hair; brown eyes, eye lid lines and brow, red mouth; wears wool suit and black tassel; white wool dress; marked France, "S/C", in a diamond shaped design. Non-ethnic.
3. "No-Name", p. 36, John and Janet Clendenien Collection. Dark-colored; molded hair in tiny curls; jointed, fully; stationary, brown glass eyes; marked France/SNF/50; 1930; ethnic.
4. "No-Name", p. 56, John and Janet Clendenien Collection. Toddler - "Poupee Nobel Doll, Unisex hair cut", brown hair wig; blue sleep eyes fully jointed; marked France/SNF/ 59 59, non-ethnic.
5. "Hottentot", p. 100, 1914-1925, celluloid, came as a pair in blue and white checked blanket; black hair, white wings; shoulder jointed; marked 8/0 - (Kewpie Reg. US. Pat 1913 Rose O'Neill, marked on the back.
6. "No-Name", p. 115, mahogany colored, 3¾" inches; shoulders jointed; rough red shirt; molded eyeballs wiht black dots; red mouth; dimples; black molded hair. Semi-Ethnic; marked, Japan enclosed in a rectangular and a circle with a geometric design.
7. "No-Name", p. 130, Black baby inside watermelon, coal-black celluloid; molded hair; painted eyes; red mouth; red brow; hip and shoulder jointed; has diaper with pin; non-ethnic; marked (trefoil).

Alexander's Rag Line, Hunter, Marsha T., 1982 C.R. Hunter Printing, Knoxville, TN.
1. Black So-Lite Baby (1942), p. C 57, Tardie Collection. Cloth,

Stockenette body, brown felt face; felt mask, brown eyes, brown hair, yarn wig, non-ethnic.

All-Bisque and Half Bisque Doll, Angione, Genevieve, 1969, Thomas Nelson and Sons, Camden, NJ and simultaneously in Toronto, CA.
1. "Mulatoo Boy", plate #22, p. 65, Brewer Collection. French - Type neck loop, 5⅝" incised on head 61 over 13. Some numbers side by side appear on the flanges (leg). Even, golden coffee color; irisless eyes, black one-stroke brows, red lips, closed mouth, open top head covered by a curly black mohair wig on a cardboard gome, joint body, decorated head dress c beads, beads on neck double strand, cloth on torso, bare chesst, shoes.
2. "Nubian Male", plate #23, p. 66, 9" pnt. black jointed body, loop strung c rubber, low gloss texture, mohair curled wig - on a cap, closed mouth, strong molded features, French style-doll.
3. "Black Male", plate #24, p. 66. 5½, peg strung, open mouth, French - Type unproportional hands and feet, very small soft brown color, curled mohair wig on a cap.
4. "Negro Boy", plate 97, p. 128, Brewer Collection. 4½ inches, hip and shoulder jointed, stiff neck, soft brown, irisless glass eyes are set, one stroke black brows, closed mouth, red nose dots, black mohair wig on a gauze cap, small plaster dome the size of a dime. Kestner used these as well as the curled wigs on cloth caps (164 5/0 on head) marked in 2 lines.

American Folk Dolls, Lavitt, Wendy, 1982, Alfred A. Knopf, New York, NY
1. Chapter entitled "Black Dolls", p. 69 - 83.

Antique Collector's Dolls, Smith, Patricia, 1975, Collector Books, Paducah, KY

1. "No-Name", p. 28, Bisque; Black male baby; 4″, jointed shoulders and hips, marked Japan.
2. "No-Name", p. 28, Bisque; Black female baby, 4″, 3 pigtails; jointed shoulders and hips, marked Japan.
3. "No-Name", p. 42, circa 1910, black, composition baby; 26″ marked AM/Germany 518-6/K-12-B-C-26.
4. "No-Name", p. 59, brown socket head; black sleep eyes; open mouth; 4 feet, marked made in German Armand Marseille 390n/D.R.G.M. 246/a/A. 2½M; 16″.
5. "No-Name", p. 59, colored baby doll; marked 39, 16″.

Barbie Dolls, Manos, Paris, Susan and Carol, 1982, Collector Books, Paducah, KY
1. Francie Doll, p. 16 (1967), brown tone; light brown eyes, red hair, non-ethnic.
2. Christie Doll, p. 21, (1969-1970), brown tone, talking 1969-70's, twist 1969.
3. Julia Doll, p. 20 (1969-1970), brown tone, modeled after Diane Carrol's part in TV series "Julia".

Compo Dolls, Cute and Collectible, Vol. II, Shoemaker, Rhonda, 1973, Top Copy Center, Menlo Park, CA.
1. "No-Name", p. 12, Negro 10″; composition; attributed to Madame Hendren; non-ethnic.
2. "No-Name", p. 36, brown hair; 12½″, composition, cloth body; jointed arms and legs, stationary head, marked E.I.H.C.., Inc. non-ethnic.
3. Patsy Baby (1932), p. 50, 10″ Negro baby, all compo; jointed at neck, shoulders and hip; bent arms and baby legs; molded painted hair with three black yarn pigtails, painted eyes to one side, marked; Effanbee Patsy baby.
4. Phyllis, p. 80, 13″ Negro Little Girl; all compo; jointed at shoulders, molded painted hair, painted eyes, closed mouth.

Delightful Dolls, Antique and Otherwise, Bateman, Thelma, 1966, Hobby House Press, Washington, D.C. 20044
1. "Elmira", p. 87 - top right, papier mache″ body with 34-13 incised on the back of her socket head of bisque, 5″, black irisless eyes of blown glass, stationary, mouth slightly open wtih a white substance showing to indicate teeth, dark brown mix in the bisque, not merely fired onto the head, ball and jointed including wrists, separate fingers and thumbs, wigs of fuzzy wool, peaked black eye brows. 1880's French, brown and red dress with a gathered skirt - short with matching bonnet.
2. "Black Baby", Top L., p. 87, (Mrs. Pat Schoonmaker Collection) curved legs, turtle-marked, celluloid, high gloss, dark brown, German made, jointed shoulders and hips, 3″.

Doll Collecting for Fun & Profit, Seely, Mildred & Colean, 1983, HP Books.
1. "Black Boy", Top L.; p. 22, head only MARKED: France, light brown, inset eyes, dark brown celluloid material with red lips.
2. "Black Girl", Rare French brown colored bisque, fashionably dressed in pastel colors of pink, mauve, with a below the knee dress/ruffles and matching coat c feathered hat, lg. brown irisless eyes multistroke eyebrows, non-ethnic.

*****

*Steiner Dolls/French Dolls

The Jules Nicholas Steiner Company is one of the oldest doll-making companies. It began producing dolls in 1855. The company made many different faces. There are kicking & walking dolls as well as a type referred to as the Motschmann type, Bergoin and wire-eye Steiners.

The Motschmann-type refers to a doll made with leather fabric inserts to facilitate movement. Motschmann painted these dolls in Germany in 1857. Some of the Motschmann types have squeeze-box voices.

Most Steiners can be identified by a purple cardboard pate, instead of the usual French cork pate, (a covering over the top of the head). Sometimes purple paint is evident in the joints or the toes' undersides. A purple undercoat of paint is used on the composition bodies.

The fingers are usually the same length. Some later versions can be found with twisting waists. The steiner label has a small girl with a banner for the later models after 1889. The Steiner Company made both Black and Mullatto dolls however they are rare. p. 92-93.

*****

3. "Male", bottom right, p. 106, wooden fully jointed, metal hands and feet, (Joel Ellis) mortise and tendon joints patented, painted body.
4. "Black Girl", bottom right, p. 110, composition-dark brown, molded hair, decal eyes of amber with black pupils, open-closed mouth with (1) tooth showing upper, red lips, pierced ears, glossy finish, ethnic.
5. "French Girl", (top left & middle) "**Dahliah**", Marked Bru Jne 7, black mohair wig, br.-blk paper wt. eyes, bisque head & arms/leather body and wood legs, original costume of plaid long shirt, a blouse with plaid ascot type shawl with head wrapped with matching plaid fabric/leather shoes with socks.
6. "Black Boy", 15″, p. 137, bisque head/hands, cloth body and a flange neck, original costume suspender short pants of a cream color with a red stitched shirt, side glancing paint eyes.

Dolls, Images of Love, Vol. I, Selfridge, Jim & Madalaine, 1973, Jim/Madalaine Selfrigde, 3572 Marin Dr., Irvine, CA 92705.
1. "Black Girl", (top left, Bru section), p. 1 #, (Bru Jne 7): marks on back of head circle with dot in center above words; shoulder incised (Bru Jne 7). Bru paper label on chest. Bisque lower arms/lower feet wood, brown eyes, marked Bru shoes. (Billie Nelson Tyrrell collection), non-ethnic.
2. "Brown Bisque Child", (far - left-bottom), p. 16, #100, 18″ marked incised = ¼f 1, brown eyes, animal or human hair wig. (Billie Nelson Tyrrell Collection).
3. "Baby", incised "Simon and Halbig/k* R-100 soft brown bisque, br. painted eyes, open closed mouth, brown curved baby body. (Louise McBride Collection).
4. "Negro Child", #144, p. 40, soft br. bisque flirty eyes, open mouth with (2) upper teeth, tremble tongue, incised "252 S & O" together in circle, Germany". S & O is mark found on some dolls distributed by John Bing the sole American agent for Kammer & Reinhardt. (Terry Crocheron Collection).
5. "Negro Child", #165, p. 45, "S-12 H/739//Dep". br. paper wt. eyes open mouth, pierced ears, black curly wig in pigtails, joint compo body/bisque head, upper teeth showing, (Linda Spiegel Collection).
6. "Negro" #176, p. 48 (lady), incised "1358 // Germany // Simon & Halbig // S & H // 16″ Lt. br. bisque with natural pink lips, brown eyes, no upper pnt. lashes, open mouth pierced ears, fur wig, 19″, teeth showing at top. Strong ethnic.
7. "Dark Brown Bisque Baby", #197, p. 53, 9″ br. intaglio eyes to one side, molded black hair, closed lips, dark brows compo body with light brown finger and toe nails, incised, with sunburst and "7671 - Germany" original yellow chemise. (Selfridge Collection) Ethnic.
8. "Negro Bruckner Rag Doll", #339, p. 90 Negroid features, 12″ wavy hair style, upper and lower teeth showing, lady (Billie Nelson Tyrrell) Ethnic.
9. "Black Sambo", #208, p. 56, 15″ brown sl. eyes, closed mouth, red lips, pierced ears, 5-pc. toddler compo body, original box has sunburst red, yellow paper label for neck reads, "South Seas Baby-Ges, Gesch-Made in Germany" with mark on the head (Heubach

Koppelsdorf-399-2/0-DRGM-Germany, (Billie Nelson Tyrrell Collection).

*****

Dolls and Doll-Makers, Hillier, Mary, 1968, G.P. Putnam's Son, NY
*. . . Simon & Halbig seem to have been at the forefront with new ideas and they were one of the first firms to use coloured bissque to represent dolls of other than European type; they made chocolate coloured negro heads with authentic modeling (2nd para.) p. 176.

*****

1. "Black Girl", (top line), p. 176, Simon & Halbig KR 53', 22", glass eyes, animal or human hair wig, bisque head with compo body.
2. "No-Name, p. 37, O.D. Gregg Collection, Brown-tone, open mouth; marked #2 on head.
3. "No-Name", p. 82, Josephine Wingfield Collection, papier mache; glass inset eyes, 6". Non-ethnic.
4. "No-Name", p. 111, Diane Hoffman Collection, Bisque; 6" closed mouth, painted lashes; black eyes. Non-ethnic.

Handbook of Collectible Dolls, Merrill Madeline, 1969, Woodward and Miller, Inc., Richard Merrill, 486 Main St., Melrose, MA 02176.
1. "Drema Baby", p. 37, 1924 Marks, "A.M." "Germany" (on head), brown bisque with black pnt. hair, blk. stationary eyes. Non-ethnic.
2. "Black Girl", p. 69, 5", 1900-1920, bisque brown, glass eyes, blk. mohair wig, bare ft. hat, bonnet long dress with slip showing and smock. Non-ethnic.
3. "Frozen Charlotte", p. 141, (3rd from left), 1850-1920, ceramic (china), 1-pc. body found in many sizes, Frozen Charlotte Pillar dolls. Quality varies most are undressed or have paitned-on clothes, rarer ones are dressed. Non-ethnic. *Rare - are ethnic Charlottes.
4. Milliners Models (far R-back), p. 166, 1800-1850s, Narrow waisted leather or cloth bodies with wood limbs, often found with bands of colored paper where arms and legs join body, various sizes, Black Milliners are rare. Non-ethnic.
5. "Black Lady", p. 173, small, 1880-1920, Black cloth with compo limbs, papier-mache head. Ethnic.
6. "Black Lady", p. 214, 1880-1900, cloth body with compo limbs and wax over compo head, lg. eyes glass stat., black lambskin wig, wears heeled-compos boots (original), hands and feet metal.
7. "Springfield", p. 234, wood fully jointed, 1881 Mason & Tyler, female. Non-ethnic. *Black Springfield's are rare and Black Males are even rarer by these doll makers.

Heubach's Little Characters; Dolls and Figurines, 1850-1930. Stanton, Carol, 1978, Living Dolls Limits, Enfield, MA.
1. "No-Name", p. 21, Black boy; open mouth, glass-eyes, 10617 on head; jointed. Non-ethnic.
2. "No-Name", p. 37, Negro boy, closed mouth, bisque head, red mouth, smiling, two lower teeth, composition bent limb body, marked "Heubach Koppelsdorf 414 D.R.G.M. Ethnic.
3. "No-Name", p. 38-39, Negro boy twins, lifesize, 36 inches, brown cotton bodies, bent limbs - composition, composition head, crinkly molded black hair, glass flirty eyes, smiling-two upper teeth, mark-"Germany".

Johana's Dolls, a reprint of her columns and articles, Anderton, Johana Gast 1975, Athena Publishing Company North Kansas City
1. "No-Name, p. 19, composition, molded hair with embroidery floss sprouts in the top and sides of head, painted teeth, open and/or closed mouth, 1920's-30's, 16". Ethnic-features.
2. "Lucifer", p. 19, compo head & feet, wooden sticks/string attached, 14" marionette, molded hair, red/white checked shirt, tan cotton pants with patch of skirt material, marked; (c)/Ethnic-features.
3. "No-Name", p. 20, 14" toddler with straight legs of compo, compo head with molded hair & compo hands/arms, cotton stuffed body,

painted brown, cotton print dress with matching bonnet, sleep eyes with brown decals. Non-ethnic.
4. "Cynthia", p. 20, 14", All smooth brown hard plastic, Madame Alex. Doll Co., lg. brown sleep eyes, rooted hair-black original costume, white dress with red print and navy black trim, belt buckle on front, sock/shoes of patent leather, solemn expression, non-ethnic, 1950's.
5. "No-Name", Negro Man, p. 23, 18" original caracul wig, brown paper weight eyes, open-closed mouth (no teeth), ball jointed, papier mache body - painted brown, applied ears, bisque head, RARE FRENCH Doll, blue ribbon winner, hat, shirt, overalls.
*"Negro Man" p. 22 (Ralphs Antique Dolls), OMAHA Convention October, 1972 Omaha Hilton.
6. "Brad", p. 26, from Barbie Collection - Christie's date? Molded features. Ethnic-features.
7. Doll ARTIST p.33, memo. portraits/Black leaders, *Roberta Bell* information in souvenir book of UFDC convention write: Analeene, 5000 Chicago Omaha, Neb. 68132.
8. Ventriloquist dolls p. 45, (The Antique Reporter, Nov. 1973) New releases, Willie Tyler's (Blk. doll) - "Lester" (introduced by Goldberger) - black boy doll, grin with fluffy Afro hairdo & glasses.

Jumeau Prince of Dollmakers, King, Constance 1983, Hobby House Press Cumberland, MD.
1. Emile Jumeau, p. 50, Abla Odell Collection, animal hair wig, jointed body, fixed hands, brown-tone, glass eyes, ethnic features, marked Depose' E-8-J on head, E. Jumeau Med. or 1878 Pairs on body, 18½".

Madame Alexander, Dolls on Review, Uhl, Marjorie U.S. 1981, Taylor Publishing Company, Dallas Texas.
1. "Cynthia", (1952-53), p. 49, Three sizes)15",18",23"); brown skin, head moveable, side to side, legs move, 1953 is a walker, sleep eyes. Non-ethnic.
2. "Janie", (1965), p. 128, Black, 12". Non-ethnic.

Madame are Made With Love, Uhl, Marjorie U.S. 1983, Taylor Publishing Company, Dallas Texas
1. "leslie", (1966), Black Female, 17" p. 77.
2. "Baby; Ellen", (1968), Black Baby, 14" p. 88, Mary Ellen Maxwell Collection.
3. "Victoria", p. 91, Black female baby, 20", #5852.
4. "Pussy Cat", (1969), p. 96, Black Baby 20", Cry Voice.

More Twentieth Century Dolls Anderton, Johana Gast 1974, Athena Publishing Company, North Kansas City
1. "Campbell Kid", p. 487, adv-C3, 11½, molded blk, hair & eyes, original clothes (Hughes Collection), (Horsman Doll Company). Non-ethnic.
2. "Rastus" adv-C16 p. 491, Cream of Wheat Chef, litho cloth, holding a bowl of cereal with label on bow, stripped pants solid color jacket, long sleeves, smiling, 18" (ref. TCD p. 27). Caricature features.
3. "Uncle Mose", 13½ printed features, stuffed plastic: R.T. Davis Mills/St. Joseph, Mo., changed to Aunt Jemima Mills - is now a part of Quaker Oats: "Uncle Mose"/back of feet.
4. "Baby Ellen", 14" rooted synthetic wig, brown sleep eyes, drink/wet mouth, soft vinyl head, soft satin light brown plastic body/limbs, fully jointed, original blk/white polka dot dress with knit booties, diaper & bottle, Marks: ALEXANDER/1965 on head (Rodgers Collection). Non-ethnic.
5. "Germany No-Name", head only 2½: stat. eyes - br. glass, lips with (4) teeth, c. 1894 Marks: A.M. 410/MADE IN GERMANY (Parker Collection). Ethnic.
6. "No-Name", Bisq-30 p. 611, 11" black mohair wig covered with turban, stat. brown glass eyes, pierced ears, open mouth with (4)

upper teeth, 9-pc pained brown compo body with wooden reinforcements, bisque head, stringing attaches to back of the crown with (2) - clips, Marks: 227/Dep. on head, (Meekins Collection). "Negro Child".

7. "Bye-lo Baby", BLB-10, p. 622, 15″, molded hair, painted blue eyes, closed mouth, sticky vinyl head/limbs, stuffed cloth body, original dres, Marks: Grace Storey/Putnam (on head), dress tag reads; Bye-Lo Baby, NONE GENUINE WITHOUT SIGNATURE, Grace Storey Putnam. (Burtchett Collection).

8. "Scootles", CAM-35 p. 623 14½″, molded-painted hair, and eyes, closed mouth, fully jointed, brown composition head and body, original peach romper, blue blouse and socks, 1930's. (Ortwein Collection, photo by Jackie Meekins).

9. "Colored Miss Peep", CAM-45, p. 625, 15″ molded hair, inset glassine eyes-br., closed mouth, soft-stuffed vinyl with patented joints, original clothes, 1969, Marks: USA 53/CAMEO on head (Siehl Collection).

10. "Negro Baby" Cel-52 p. 636, 11″ molded hair, pnt. eyes with white outlines, open-closes mouth with (2) pnt. teeth, fully jointed black celluloid. Marks-30 on head and body with bird head design.

11. "Negro dolls", catalog p. 638, 4½, 2 styles, jointed arms, assorted color shirts, came 2 doz. box originally, cat. #64-0812 Celluloid, Ethnic/Caricature.

12. "Negro Dolls", 3 styles, 7″ bell-hops and girl dolls with shirt dresses, some with jointed arms/legs doz/box (64-0992 cat. #). Ethnic/caricature.

13. Pickaninny", catalog, p. 640, 3½″ jointed arms, assorted color silk chenille costume hat/dress celluloid, 2 doz. box, Ethnic/caricature. (Cat #2F9793).

14. "Negro Doll", catalog, p. 640, "Star Value" 3½″ jointed arms/legs, cardboard melon box, 3 doz. corrugated box cat #2F9790.

15. "Colored head", CH1-19 p. 645, 2″ head only, white eyes, red lips (Parker Collection). Ethnic.

16. "Rachel", COM-R1 p. 665, 3½″ molded pnt. bisque, swivel neck, from comic strip by Frank O. King. (Ortwein Collection), photo by Jackie Meekins. Caricature.

17. "Negro Baby", DC-3, p. 675. 20″ br. sleep eyes, drink/wet - mouth, soft vinyl head, rigid plastic body/limbs, tiny red earrings: Mfr: Dee Cee (Campbell Collection). Non-ethnic.

18. "Colored Grumpy", F & B-58, p. 720 Marks: EFFANBEE (Stewart Collection) 11½″ pnt. hair/molded with floss braids, pnt. side glance eyes, closed mouth, compo with deep shoulder, head & limbs stuffed cloth body, made 1912-1939, Ethnic.

19. "Colored Patsyette", F & B-89 p. 731 9″ molded-pnt. amber side glance eyes, colored mouth, fully jointed, brown compo body, original clothes cape with small cloth over front torso. Non-ethnic.

20. "Colored Ann", F & B-102 p.734 21″ black wig, human hair, brown sleep eyes, pnt. mouth, fully jointed, compo, 1935. Marks: EFFANBEE/ANNE SHIRLEY ON SHOULDERS (photo by Barbara McLaughlin, owner), dress short with wide lapels puff sleeves shot with gathered bodice raised decoration on lower part of entire bodice and sleeves collar-1 patch.

21. "Lorrie Lee", 8¾″ rooted black saran braids, pnt blk. eyes, closed mouth, fully/jnt. br. vinyl body, original windowpane stockings, short dress with short sleeves, printed bodice with straps & plain top, plastic shoes molded, Marks 23/LORRIE DOLL/1969 on head Made IN HONG KONG on back (Mason Collection).

22. "African Baby" Heu-17b.p.790, 8½″ pnt. eyes, closed mouth, post earrings ring on left andle. Marks: Heubach-Koppelsdorf (McLaughlin Collection), purchases in Cuba 1936. Ethnic.

23. "Snowflake", Hitt-1. p. 790, 3¾″, molded-pnt. bisque, glass dome eyes, blk floating pupils. Marks: SNOWFLAKE, Corp. By/OSCAR HITT, Germany. (Swift Collection). Caricature.

24. "Black Doll", Hors-74, p. 802, molded-pnt. features. can't Break

'EM Head, compo hands, soft body & limbs, Horsman Doll (Playthings June 1913, Nov. 1914). Ethnic.

25. "Bootsie", 12½″ rooted blk. synth. hair, brown sleep eyes, closed mouth, soft vinyl head, arms, hrd vinyl legs, body. Marks: 1907, 13 eye, T125, 3, C. HORSMAN DOLLS INC. 1969 (Wardell Collection).

26. "Colored Crissy", IDL-152, p. 868, 18½″ rooted blk. growing hair, blk. sleep eyes with lashes, open - closed smile, soft plastic head rigid plastic body & limbs, apple green lace dress, panties, shoes, pink ribbon and comb. Marks: 1968, IDEAL TOY CORP/GH-17-H129; 1969, IDEAL TOY CORP./GH-18-U.S.PAT. 3, 182,976 on (r) hip (Johana Gast Anderton Collection). Non-ethnic.

27. "Belly Button Baby", IDL 162-b, p. 871, rooted blk hair, pnt. brown eyes, closed mouth, tongue sticks out corner, soft vinyl head, limbs hard plastic body, body moves when button pushed, *six different heads. "Glad" Black doll (female) "So Happy" (boy also). Marks: 1970 IDEAL TOY CORP. E9-5-H159, HONG KONG (head), IDEAL TOY CORP. HONG KONG, 2A-0156 (body), (Anderton Collection).

28. "Small Stuff", Jol-8, p. 886, Topsy, 14½″, pnt./rooted synthetic hair, brown sleep eyes with lashes, closed mouth, fully jointed vinyl, short dress, bibbed top, lace trim, bib-top, tag on arm with anme MARKS: 7/JOLLY TOYS INC. 1960, tag reads Jolly's Small Stuff¢, TRADEMARK A PRODUCTION OF JOLLY TOYS INC. NEW YORK N.Y. (Anderton Collection). Semi-Ethnic.

29. "Colored Doll", Lor-1, p. 926 21½″ rooted synt. black hair, sleep eyes, open closed mouth, tongue, brown vinyl 1 head, limbs, cloth body, pink silk dress, Marks: LORRIE DOLL COMP., 1962, (Anderton Collection).

30. "Piccaninny", 10½″ rooted blk. & brown streaked hair, sleep eyes, closed mouth, fully jointed, soft oil, dark brown body, bent baby legs, cloth and string loincloth, caries paper boomarang reads: PICCANINNY; box decor with pictures of Australian people and animals. UInmarked, (Anderton Collection) Metti (Australian Mfg.) Carry a compl. line from brides Aborigine people (Black Australians). Ethnic.

31. "Topsy-Turvy", Mult-12 p. 962, 14½″, mohair wigs, pnt. eyes, litho cloth, hard molded heads, cotton dresses (black side with printed dress) long sleeves, patented July 8, 1901 by Albert Bruckner; distributed by Horsman. Ethnic.

32. "Topsy-Turvy", Mult-14 p.962 7½″, blk cotton floss hair over molded hair (on Black doll) with pnt. features/head swivels (White doll-head stat. no floss hair) Unmarked (Stewart Collection). Non-ethnic.

33. "Crawling Baby", Nov. 28, p.987, 10″ molded-pnt. hair, pnt. blk eyes, open-closed mouth, 1 pc. plaster compo, diaper molded-to hold some additioal attachment (i.e., ornamentation) also available in White version.

34. "Saucy Walkers" Ped 7 a-b p. 999, pair-girl/boy twins by Pedigree a British Mfg. Co. (International Model Aircraft LTD. Merton, London, S.W. 19 England) roving eyes, says "Ma-Ma no size given.

35. Colored Terri Lee & Jerri Lee Pers-L4 a-b p. 1018, 16″ blk wigs, pnt. brown eyes, closed mouth, fully jointed hard plastic, original clothes, boy-short pants, stripped Jacket long sleeves; girls-short dress, waist bodice, short, sleeve top, bow in top of hair, shoes, socks for both. Non-ethnic, Marks: TERRI LEE on backs (O'Rourke Collection).

36. "Jackie Robinson", Pers-R3 p. 1026, 13″ pnt. features, fully jointed, compo, all original, blk./white, Brooklyn Dodgers' uniform, 1950; baseball bat reads: JACKIE ROBINSON. *An identical doll wears uniform with (42) on back of jersey: bat reads: GENUINE/RICHIE/AHSBURN/LOUISVILLE   SLUGGER/BATS/HILLERICH S. BRADSBY & COMPANY/LOUISVILLE Ky. (Siehl Collection). Ethnic.

*The Remco Brown - Eyed Series

In 1968, a young Negro artist, Annuel McBurroughs supervised design of the Brown - Eye line for Remco. As the first authentic line of Black dolls to be put on the market, Remco advertised the Brown-Eye dolls in *Time, Newsweek, and Ebony* magazines, as well as arranging for their appearance on television's Johnny Carson Show, Merv Griffin Show, and the Huntley-Brinkley Show. The dolls are ethnicaly correct; however they did not sell well in spite of the big "sell job" and were shortly discontinued. Dolls included in the Brown-Eye series are:

Polly Puff	Jumpsey	Tiny Thumbles
Tumbling Tomboy	Billy	Baby-Know-it-All
Bunny Baby	Baby whistle	Growing Sally
Twins	Tina	Li'l Winking Winny
Baby		
Grow-A-Tooth	Kewpie	Baby Laugh-A-Lot
Tippy Tumbles		

37. "Brown-Eye Winking Winny", Remco-21 p. 1064, 15″ push button & doll winks one eye. Marks: SE10/REMCO IND. INC./1968. (Wardell Collection), Vinyl; rooted blk. hair, fully jointed, closed mouth, lg. brown eyes, smiling expression, jumper dress with turtle neck blouse, chain on neck.

38. "Br.-Eye Baby Grow-A-Tooth", REm-22 p. 1064, 15″ rooted synt. hair, br. eyes, open - closed mouth with (1) top tooth, hard plastic and vinyl, fully jointed battery operated, Marks: REMCO IND. INC. 1968, *(1968 CAt Ill.).

39. "Brown Eye Tina", Rem23ab p. 1064 (2) 15″, (girl) 16″ (boy) rooted black hair, brown sleep eyes, fully jointed, vinyl and hard plastic 1969 cat. illustration.

40. "Brown-eye Tumbling Tomboy", Rem-24 p. 1064, (No size listed), black rooted hair (2-long braids with bangs, dome shaped cap/no bib, checkered long pants with sleeveless shell top, hard plastic & vinyl (cat. ill. 1969).

41. "Brown-Eye Twins" Rem-25 p. 1064, 9″, molded black painted hair, pnt br. eyes, drink/wet mouth, fully jointed, (cat ill).

42. "Brown Eye Baby Know It All", Rem-26 p. 1065, Marks: 2955/17/Eye/New/E6 REMCO IND. INC./1969, 17″ rooted synth. black hair, brown sleep eyes, fully jointed also hip & knee jointed, hard plastic body and vinyl, checkered rumper suit-long with bid, shakes head "yes"/"no", jumps up and down in chair if she sees a picture of something that she likes. High chair included.

43. "Brown-Eye Growing Sally" Rem-27 p. 1065, 6¼″ rooted black thick hair, straight legs and arms, closed mouth with smiling expresion, possibly joint at shoulder/hps cat. il 1969.

44. "Brown-Eye Bunny Baby", Rem-28 p. 1065 18″ rooted blk. hair, stat. eyes/br., open-closed mouth, fully jointed, vinyl & hard plastic, *blow bunny whistle locket and doll moves arms/legs and stops by herself. Doll also rides a bunny-swing when the whistle is blown. Marks: A.f. 3222 BRS/E 15 (in a square)/REMCO. IND. INC. 1969. (cat. ill. 1969).

45. "Lady", Roy-3, p. 1076, 19½″ rooted blk synt. hair in bun-style, amber sleep eyes, closed mouth, fully jointed-vinly, gown of various shades of pink, high heeled shoes, nylon stockings, rhinestone choker style necklace, earrings, 1950's. Marks: 14 R., ROYAL DOLL COMPANY, courtesy of Nita's House of Dolls. Semi-Ethnic.

46. "Emma Sue", 2 photos/Roy-5 p. 1976 (Author's Collection), Semi-Ethnic, 18″, black saran wig, brown sleep eyes, lashes, closed mouth, fully jointed, brown hard plastic walker body, all original embossed cotton dress, hat with tag on left arm and cloth purse with draw strings, on right arm: THE ROYAL DOLL MFG. CO., INC./NEW YORK EST, 1914 doll is unmarked.

47. "The Sasha Family", Cora, 16″, Caleb 16″, and Black Baby 12″, rooted black afro hair, pnt. eyes, closed mouth, rigid vinyl, fully jointed, various costumes, *Originated by Sasha Morgenthaler of Switzerland, Mfr: Sash Dolls, Serie, England, Marks: Tag on wrist; SASHA; some dolls are unmarked and others marked SASHA/SERIS (Campbell Collection). Non-Ethnic.

48. "Bendable Figure", Sch-1 p. 1092, All solid vinyl, pnt. features and clothes. Marks: SCHLEICH'S BIEBEFGURNE on right foot; MADE IN WEST GERMANY, J.N.U. AUSLPAT on left foot. (Swift Collection). Ethnic.

49. "Lil Souls", 6″,7″,10″, Ethnic, SH1-1 a-d, p. 1099, (Hartwell Collection), curly yarn hair, black eyes, pink mouths, stuffed bodies, baby in bib, short romper suit, "Sis" in short flaring stripped dress with head band, "Wilkie" in shirt & blouse, "Natra" in short pants with logn sleeve shirt, Mfg: Shindana, Division of Mattel Inc.

50. "timpo Toys", Tim 2 a, 2 a-j p. 1114, 2 Black dolls no size given or other descriptions can be determined from the cat. ill. *Toy Trader, Sept. 1943), *Ethnic Toy Exporters, Ltd. (London?).*

51. "Colored Walker", Unee-25, p. 1121, 35″ rooted black hair, amber sleep eyes, closed mouth, soft vinyl head, arms, hard plastic body, legs, fully jointed, 1960, Marks: UNEEDA/37 (Siehl Collection). Semi-Ethnic. Uneeda Doll Co./New York founded 1917 to present.

52. "Colored Baby", p. 1128, unmarked 62, 4¼″, pnt. br.-side glance eyes, red nostrils, pnt. mouth with (2) teeth, papier mache, Ethnic/caricature, linen dress/collar, (Burtchett Collection).

53. "Topsy Baby", unmarked-101, p. 1136, 16″ floss braids, pnt. black side-glance eyes with white highlights, open-closed mouth (2) pnt. teeth, stuffed cloth body, print dress with cloth tied around chest over the dress, 1930 (Wardell Collection), Ethnic.

54. "Girl", 13″ pnt. brown side glance eyes, closed mouth, deep molded black curly hair, compo, fully jointed, 1930's (Thomspon Collection).

55. "African Baby", crated by Piramonie (Playthings, Nov. 1915), *War Dolls* Ethnic/caricature, War-lc p. 1160.

*Dolls Made by Refugee Artist, Working in N.Y. many refugee artists supported themselves by making dolls. War dolls may be divided into several subcategories. There are commercial dolls designed to promote or capitalize on patriotism during a national crisis. There are dolls created by refugees not only in an effort to support themselves but often with a real attempt at raising funds to asist other refugees from war torn countries or to return needed supplies and encouragement to suffer relatives and attempts by artists to make serious statements about their times and situation in doll form.

Often such efforts received the assistance of an established doll manufacturer or the workers were taken into firms. Another purpose was served since material for dolls during wartime is usually in short supply and these refuee toymakers were adept at creating dolls and toys with minimum resources. Their creations were double welcomed in view of the shortages of dolls and toys; in England for example, second-hand toy exchanges and sales were the regular routine during both wars.

A program sponsored by the Red Cross Institute in the reconstruction of the crippled soldier advocated the use by industry of physically disabled veterans in selected industrial positions.

The study pointed out various ways in which men who had lost limbs or suffered other handicaps could be taught new work or could adjust former skills to new needles.

The toy industry responded to the plea of Douglas C. McMurtie, director of the Red Cross program. Many war veterans began the long road back with jobs in the doll and toy factories of this nation. p. 1160.

More Twentieth Century Dolls, Vol. 1 A-H 2nd Printing, Anderton, Johana Gast 1979, Wallace-Homestead Book Company, 1912 Grand Avenue Des Moines, Iowa 50305.

1. "Sambo-The Nigger Baby", non-ethnic, Hors-45, p. 794, 12,15″, compo head, spring jointed body, "The first completely jointed doll ever made in the U.S. sold for $8.50 and $13.50 per dozen. (Playthings, April 1910) copy. E.I. Horsman and Aetna Doll & Toy Company. Hors-33 E.I. Horsman Jr. 1918, Hors-34 E.I. Horsman 1918, Hors-38 "New FActory of E.I. Horsman and Aetna Doll com-

pany Layfayette Street, New York where the Horsman bisque dolls are made".
2. "Black Doll", Hors-74 p. 802, molded-pnt. features, "Can't Break 'em Head", compo hands, soft body and limbs, straw-wide brim hat, quarter length pants with attached suspenders, shirt with ankle shoes, No size available. (Playthings, June 1913, Nov. 1914).

Nancy Ann Storybook Dolls, Miller, Marjorie A. 1980, Hobby House Press, Cumberland, Md.
1. Judy, p. 125, Bisque; arms and legs jointed, mohair wig, painted eyes, marked on back, Judy Ann, USA 5".
2. "No-Name", p. 169, (1948), plastic arms and legs and head, moveable, (not on 3½" or 4½", inches in size); Marked story book dolls, U.S.A., Trademark, REG.

Schoenhut Dolls & Toys, Manos, Susan 1976, Collector Books Paducah Kentucky
1. "No-Name", Negro Man p. 24, p.71.
2. "No-Name", Two Black Male Dolls "Dudes" p.31.
3. BLACK Billikin, small, wood, p.65.

Price Guide Listing

Antique Collector's Dolls, Volume I. Smith, Patricia, 1978. Collector Books, Paducah, Kentucky.
Antique Doll Price Guide. Third Edition. Leuzzi, Marlene and Kershner, Robert J., 1975. 133 Westward Drive, Carte Madera, California
Doll Values - Antique to Modern, Volumes I, II and III. Smith, Patricia, 1978-1982. Collector Books, Paducah, Kentucky.
Horsman Dolls, 1950-1970. Gibbs, Patikii, 1985. Collector Books, Paducah, Kentucky.
The Knopf Collectors' Guides to American Antiques, "Dolls". Lavitt, Wendy, 1983. Alfred A. Knopf, New York, New York.
The Kovels' Antiques and Collectibles Price List. Kovel, Ralph and Terry, 1984. Crown Publishers, Inc., New York.
Modern Dolls, Volumes I-V. Smith, Patricia, 1975-1983. Collector Books, Paducah, Kentucky.

Nineteenth Edition Warman's Antiques and Their Prices. Rinker Harry L., 1985. Warman Publishing Co., Inc., Elkins Park, Pennsylvania.
Official 1985 Price Guide to Antique and Modern Dolls. Hudgeons, Thomas E. III, 1985. House of Collectibles, Inc., Orlando, Florida.
Price Guide to Dolls. Miller, Robert W., 1982. Wallace Homestead Book Company, Des Moines, Iowa.
Sixth Blue Book Dolls and Values. Foulke, Jan, 1984. Hobby House Press, Inc., Cumberland, Maryland.
The Standard Antique Doll Identification and Value Guide. Schroeder, Bill, 1976. Collector Books, Paducah, Kentucky.
The Warner Collector's Guide to Dolls. Bach, Jean, 1982. Warner Books, Inc., New York.

Doll Companies Which Carried A Line of Black Dolls

A
A & H Doll Mfg. Corp.
Ace Toy Mfg. Co.
Adanta Novelties Corp.
Admiration Toy Co., Inc.
Alexander Doll Co., Inc.
Allied Doll and Toy Corp.
Allied-Grand Doll Mfg. Co., Inc.
Allison Corp.
American Merchandise Distributor
American Tortoise Inc.
AMSCO Industries Inc.
Arcadia Doll Co., Inc.
Armand Marseille
Art Fabric
Artistic Doll Co.
Artwood Toy Mfg. Co., Inc.
Associated Syndicate
Astor Doll & Toy Mfg. Co.
Atci Doll and Novelty
Aurora Dolls

B
Henry S. Beach Co.
Berkeley, Eddy
Blumberg H.J. Co., Inc.
Brechner Dan Co., Inc.
Bru Jne

C
Cameo Doll Products Co., Inc.
Martha Chase, "Chase Dolls"
Chic Dolls and Toy Co.

Chuck and Columbia Doll Corp.
Colombo Doll Inc.
Colpack Chenille & Novelty Co.
Common Wealth Plastics Corp.

D
Dakin R. and Co.
Dandee Doll Mfg. Co.
Deans Rag Book of London
Doll Bodies Inc.
Dolls of Hollywood

E
Ecco Industries, Limited
Effanbee Doll Corp.
Joel Ellis
Embree Mfg. Co.
Empire Doll Co.
Eugene Doll & Novelty Co., Inc.
Everglad Doll Co.

F
F. Gautier
F. Gesland
Fiberoid Doll Products Co.
Flagg and Co., Inc.
Fleischaker and Baun, Inc.
Francessee Doll Co.
Frisch Products Corp.

G
Galoob Lewis
Goldberger Doll Mfg. Co., Inc.

H
Halbig
J. Halpern

M. Hardy Co.
Heubach/Koppelsdorf
Holgate Brothers Co.
E.I. Horsman
Horsman Dolls Inc.

I
Ideal Toy Corp.
International Affiliates Co., Inc.

J
Jay Zee Doll Hand Co.
Jaymar Specialty Co.
Jolly Toys Inc.
Jumeau Doll Co.

K
K B Doll Corp.
Kandel Toy & Novelty Co.
Kaysam Corporation of America
Kaystan Pageant Doll Co., Inc.
Kenco Mfg. Co., Inc.
Kestner (JDK)
Knight Toy and Novelty Corp.
Knoepfler

L
Larami Corp.
A.L. Larimer
Leslie-Henry Co., Inc.
Levenson Julius Inc.
Libby-Majorette Doll Corp.
Lovable Toys Inc.
Lovee Doll & Toy Co.
Lujon Sun Tan - Colored Doll Co.

M
M C Doll Co.
Madewell Doll Products Co.
M.G.M. Doll Co.
Manomatic Novelty Corp.
Mason and Taylor
Mattel, Inc.
Melbar Toy Co.
Mercer Doll Mfg. Co.
Milliners Models
Milpan Crafts
Monarch Doll Products Co.
My-Toy Co.

N
Nancy Ann Storybook Dolls Co.
Nasco Doll Co., Inc.
Natural Doll Co., Inc.
Noveloid Co.
Nippon

O
Karl Ohlbaum Co.

P
P & M Doll Co., Inc.
Peggy Ann Doll Clothes, Inc.
Plastic Molded Arts Corp.
President Novelty & Jewelry Co.
Grace S. Putnam

R
Red Seal Novelty Co.
Remco Industries, Inc.
Rex Doll and Toy Corp.
Roberta Doll Co., Inc.

Rosemary Dolls Mfg. Co., Inc.
Rosette Doll Co.
Rubin Doll Parts Corporated (Doll Heads)

S
SFBJ Paris
S & H
Schoenhut
Frank Scoparino Co.
Shackman B. and Co.
Sherman Doll & Toy Corp.
Shindana Toys Division, Operation Boostrap Inc.
Skippy Doll Corp.
Standard Doll Co.
Strauss F.J. Co., Inc.
Sun Rubber Co.

T
Tannenbaum Leonard
Topper Corporated
Trego Co.
Treasure Industries, Inc.
Toy Furniture Shop
Toy Tinkers, Inc.

U
Uneeda Doll Co.

V
Vogue Dolls, Inc.

W
I.B. Wolfset and Co.

Two Important Tools For The
Astute Antique Dealer, Collector and Investor

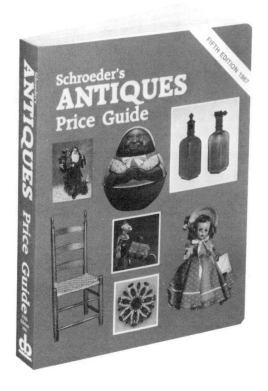

Schroeder's Antiques Price Guide

The very best low cost investment that you can make if you are really serious about antiques and collectibles is a good identification and price guide. We publish and highly recommend **Schroeder's Antiques Price Guide**. Our editors and writers are very careful to seek out and report accurate values each year. We do not simply change the values of the items each year but start anew to bring you an entirely new edition. If there are repeats, they are by chance and not by choice. Each huge edition (it weighs 3 pounds!) has over 50,000 descriptions and current values on 608 - 8½x11 pages. There are hundreds and hundreds of categories and even more illustrations. Each topic is introduced by an interesting discussion that is an education in itself. Again, no dealer, collector or investor can afford not to own this book. It is available from your favorite bookseller or antiques dealer at the low price of $11.95. If you are unable to find this price guide in your area, it's available from Collector Books, P.O. Box 3009, Paducah, KY 42001 at $11.95 plus $1.00 for postage and handling.

Flea Market Trader

Bargains are pretty hard to come by these days -- especially in the field of antiques and collectibles, and everyone knows that the most promising sources for those seldom-found under-priced treasures are flea markets. To help you recognize a bargain when you find it, you'll want a copy of the *Flea Market Trader*--the only price guide on the market that deals exclusively with all types of merchandise you'll be likely to encounter in the marketplace. It contains not only reliable pricing information, but the *Flea Market Trader* will be the first to tune you in to the market's newest collectible interests -- you will be able to buy before the market becomes established, before prices have a chance to escalate! You'll not only have the satisfaction of being first in the know, but you'll see your investments appreciate dramatically. You will love the format. Its handy 5½"x8½" size will tuck easily into pocket or purse. Its common sense organization along with detailed index makes finding your subject a breeze. There's tons of information and hundreds of photos to aid in identification. It's written with first-hand insight and an understanding of market activities. It's reliable, informative, comprehensive; it's a bargain! From Collector Books, P.O. Box 3009 Paducah, Kentucky 42001. $8.95 plus $1.00 postage and handling.

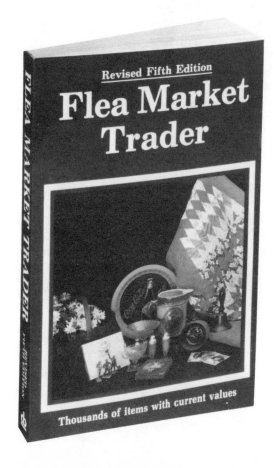

Schroeder's Antiques Price Guide

Schroeder's Antiques Price Guide has climbed its way to the top in a field already supplied with several well-established publications! The word is out, *Schroeder's Price Guide* is the best buy at any price. Over 500 categories are covered, with more than 50,000 listings. But it's not volume alone that makes Schroeder's the unique guide it is recognized to be. From ABC Plates to Zsolnay, if it merits the interest of today's collector, you'll find it in Schroeder's. Each subject is represented with histories and background information. In addition, hundreds of sharp original photos are used each year to illustrate not only the rare and the unusual, but the everyday "fun-type" collectibles as well -- not postage stamp pictures, but large close-up shots that show important details clearly.

Each edition is completely re-typeset from all new sources. We have not and will not simply change prices in each new edition. All new copy and all new illustrations make Schroeder's THE price guide on antiques and collectibles.

The writing and researching team behind this giant is proportionately large. It is backed by a staff of more than seventy of Collector Books' finest authors, as well as a board of advisors made up of well-known antique authorities and the country's top dealers, all specialists in their fields. Accuracy is their primary aim. Prices are gathered over the entire year previous to publication from ads and personal contacts. Then each category is thoroughly checked to spot inconsistencies, listings that may not be entirely reflective of actual market dealings, and lines too vague to be of merit. Only the best of the lot remains for publication. You'll find *Schroeder's Antiques Price Guide* the one to buy for factual information and quality.

No dealer, collector or investor can afford not to own this book. It is available from your favorite bookseller or antiques dealer at the low price of $12.95. If you are unable to find this price guide in your area, it's available from Collector Books, P. O. Box 3009, Paducah, KY 42001 at $12.95 plus $2.00 for postage and handling.

8½ x 11, 608 Pages $12.95